SEARCHING ISSUES

Searching
Issues

NICKY GUMBEL

KINGSWAY PUBLICATIONS
EASTBOURNE

ISBN 0 85476 461 5

Produced by Bookprint Creative Services
P.O. Box 827, BN21 3YJ, England for
KINGSWAY PUBLICATIONS LTD
Lottbridge Drove, Eastbourne, E Sussex BN23 6NT.
Printed in Great Britain

Contents

Preface

There is currently an explosion of interest in spiritual matters. It is difficult to get away from TV programmes and newspaper articles concerned with the search for meaning and purpose, life after death and the existence of God. Among these, many are taking a new look at Christianity.

While discussing the Christian faith, especially with those who are not Christians, I have found that a number of questions are raised time and again. Some of these I have looked at in *Questions of Life*. In this book, however, I want to look at those issues which are usually seen as objections to the Christian faith.

On the Alpha course, which is designed to be of help to people with such objections, we give talks based on the material in *Questions of Life*. It is often in the discussion groups afterwards that objections are raised. Those on the course may agree with much of what is being said in the talk, but they often say, 'What about . . .?' In this book I have set out the seven issues most often raised, in descending order of frequency. They are searching issues both in the sense that they are asked by those searching for the truth and in the sense that they are demanding and difficult to answer.

The issues of suffering and other religions are over-whelmingly the most common objections to the Christian faith. Sex before marriage is usually raised sometime later in the course and is often the main reason in our congregation why people delay becoming Christians. It can be seen more as a moral objection than an intellectual one. The other four issues are not brought up so regularly, but they are nevertheless raised from time to time. An increasing number of people have been involved in the New Age movement and want to work out a Christian view of it. Others are either homosexually orientated them-selves, or have friends who are, and are concerned to know what the Christian attitude to homosexuality is. The objection that science and the Christian faith conflict is less frequently raised now, but it is still an issue for some. The final chapter is on the Trinity, which is often an issue for those who have been involved in the cults, as well as those with perhaps a more philo-sophical disposition.

Each subject is vast and complex. Every one of the issues raises major theological questions. Obviously, all the matters cannot be dealt with in a few pages. Each chapter is an attempt to summarise some of the main arguments and suggest practical guidelines.

I would like to thank all those who have helped me with their comments on the drafts of this book and especially Jo Glen, Patricia Hall, Helena Hird, the Revd Chris Ash, David Sinclair, the Revd Graham S. Tomlin, Chris Simmonds, Tom Smiley, Tamsen Carter, Jon Soper and Dr Roland Werner. Finally, I would like to thank Philippa Pearson Miles for the astonishing patience, speed and dedication with which she has typed the numerous manuscripts.

1
Why Does God Allow Suffering?

A young New Yorker named Glenn Chambers had a lifelong dream to work for God in Ecuador. At the airport on the day of departure, he wanted to send a note to his mother but he didn't have time to buy a card. He noticed a piece of paper on the terminal floor and picked it up. It turned out to be an advertisement with "Why?" spread across it. He scribbled his note around the word "Why?". That night his aeroplane exploded into the fourteen thousand foot Colombian peak El Tablazo. When his mother received the note after the news of his death, the question burned up at her from the page ... "Why?".

The issue of suffering is the most frequently raised objection to the Christian faith. We are constantly confronted by suffering. 'The fact of suffering undoubtedly constitutes the single greatest challenge to the Christian faith, and has been in every generation. Its distribution and degree appear to be entirely random and therefore unfair.'[1]

First, we see suffering on a global scale. There are natural disasters: earthquakes, famines and floods. The suffering that results is often pervasive and arbitrary. In this century the two world wars have focused our attention on global suffering in an acute form. As well as these major wars, there has hardly ever been a time when there is no smaller war going on, somewhere in the world.

Secondly, we see community tragedies. One of the worst disasters in Britain was in Aberfan on 21st October 1966, when a huge coal-tip collapsed and devastated Pantglas primary school, killing 116 children and 28 adults. Almost daily we read or hear of plane crashes, sinking ships or some other disaster affecting the lives of hundreds of people.

Thirdly, suffering at an individual level affects us all to a greater or lesser extent. There is the suffering of bereavement, sickness, handicap, broken relationships, unhappy marriages, involuntary singleness, depression, loneliness, abject poverty, persecution, rejection, unemployment, injustice, fierce temptation and disappointment. Suffering can come in an endless variety of forms and no human being is immune.

It is worth noting that suffering is not a problem for all religions. It is an acute problem for the Judeo-Christian tradition because we believe that God is both good and all-powerful. C. S. Lewis stated the opposing argument succinctly: 'If God were good, He would wish to make His creatures perfectly happy, and if God were almighty, He would be able to do what He wished. But the creatures are not happy. Therefore, God lacks either goodness, or power, or both.'[2]

Theologians and philosophers have wrestled for centuries with the problem of suffering and no one has ever come up with a simple and complete solution. The Bible is primarily a practical book and it never addresses this issue systematically in a philosophical way. What we see are a number of approaches to the problem, all the way through from

Genesis to Revelation. There seem to be four main overlapping insights, and we shall look at each of them in turn.

Human freedom

Suffering is not part of God's original created order (Genesis 1-2). There was no suffering in the world before humanity rebelled against God. There will be no suffering when God creates 'a new heaven and a new earth' (Revelation 21). There will be no more crying and no more pain. Suffering only entered the world as a result of the fact that Adam and Eve sinned. It is, therefore, an alien intrusion in God's world. If all suffering is a result of sin, directly or indirectly, why did God allow sin to enter the world?

He did so because he loves us and wanted to give us free will. Love is not love if it is forced; it can only be love if there is a real choice. God gave human beings the choice and the freedom to love or not to love. Given this freedom, men and women from the beginning have chosen to break God's laws and the result has been suffering. Again, as C. S. Lewis puts it:

> It would, no doubt, have been possible for God to remove by miracle the results of the first sin ever committed by a human being; but this would not have been much good unless He was prepared to remove the results of the second sin, and of the third, and so on forever. If the miracles ceased, then sooner or later we might have reached our present lamentable situation: if they did not, then a world, thus continually underpropped and corrected by Divine interference, would have been a world in which nothing important ever depended on human choice, and in which choice itself would soon cease from

the certainty that one of the apparent alternatives before you would lead to no results and was therefore not really an alternative.[3]

Some of the suffering we endure is the result of *our own sin*. At times, suffering is the inevitable consequence of breaking God's law. There are physical laws of nature; for example, if we put our hand in the fire it gets burned. In this context, pain acts as an early warning system and protection when we exercise wrong choices. There are also moral laws. God made a world built on moral foundations and there is a natural connection between sin and its consequences. If a person abuses drugs, drug addiction may be the consequence. If we drink excessively, we may eventually suffer from alcoholism. If someone drinks and drives a car recklessly and injures himself, his injuries are partially the result of his sin. In a similar way, selfishness, greed, lust, arrogance and bad temper often lead to broken relationships and unhappiness of one sort or another.

Sometimes God actively judges sin in this life. The biblical flood is an example of suffering on a global scale caused by sin, resulting in God's judgement. When 'the Lord saw how great man's wickedness on the earth had become, and that every inclination of the thoughts of his heart was only evil all the time . . . his heart was filled with pain' (Genesis 6: 5-6). In the case of Sodom and Gomorrah, a community disaster was caused by God's judgement of sin. At other times we see God's judgement on an individual's sin (2 Kings 5: 27; Luke 1: 20; John 5: 14; Acts 5: 1-11; 1 Corinthians 11: 30). (For further discussion of the difference between the inevitable consequences of sin and God's active judgement on sin see Chapter 5 under the heading 'Is AIDS the judgement of God on homosexual practice?'.)

It is important to stress that not all suffering is the direct result of our own sin. Job's friends thought Job's suffering must be the result of his sin – but they were wrong (Job 42: 7-8). Jesus expressly repudiates the automatic link between sin and suffering (John 9: 1-3). He also points out that natural disasters are not necessarily a form of punishment from God (Luke 13: 1-5). The apostle Peter draws a distinction between suffering as a result of our own sin ('a beating for doing wrong' – 1 Peter 2: 20) and suffering which has no connection with our sin ('unjust suffering' – v 19) or suffering 'for doing good' (v 20).

While it may be appropriate for us to examine our own hearts when we are suffering, we need to be very careful about making judgements about why others are suffering. Church leader David Watson, who died of cancer at the age of fifty, pointed out the dangers of making judgements on others:

> The danger about coupling suffering with sin is that the sick person may often feel guilty anyway. Many times I have talked with those who are seriously ill, and I have found them anxiously wondering what they had done to bring about their condition. They blame themselves; or if they cannot live with that, they project their guilt on to others or God. It's someone's fault! The trouble is that either feelings of guilt, which are often imaginary, or direct accusations, which are often unfair, only encourage the sickness. Both hinder healing.
>
> Yet I know how easy this is. Sometimes I have thought of my asthma or cancer as being punishment for sin. I remember with shame many foolish things I have done in the past, and with a fairly sensitive conscience it

is not hard to feel both guilty and condemned. The positive side is that every affliction has caused me to search deeply within my heart and to repent of every sinful action or attitude that I could discover. I have known many people who have been dramatically healed following such repentance together with the experience of God's forgiveness. It is no bad thing, therefore, to consider carefully our life in the sight of God in order to know the joy and freedom of his love.

At the same time, the negative side of all this comes when such heart-searching leads to nagging and unhealthy feelings of guilt, and perhaps to a very poor image of God. Is it conceivable, when we see Jesus healing the sick and forgiving the sinful, that God should say, 'Ah, there's David Watson. He slipped up rather badly last month so I'll afflict him with asthma for the next twenty years'? Or later, 'He's upset me again, so this time I'll destroy him with cancer'? Such thoughts are not only ridiculous; they are almost blasphemous, and utterly alien to a God of infinite love and mercy as we see him so clearly in Jesus.[4]

Much of the suffering in the world is the result of *other people's sin*. This is true of many global and community disasters. So much suffering is caused by war; which is always the result of human sin, even if the sin is often on both sides. Much of the starvation in the world is caused by the unequal distribution of the world's resources or by civil war or some other human sin. Even the Aberfan disaster was not a 'natural' one. A five-month enquiry headed by Lord Justice Edmund Davies ruled that the Coal Board was responsible for the disaster. As one woman who contributed to the disaster fund wrote: 'I raged against

God, but then I realised it had happened because of man's greed and incompetence.'[5]

Likewise, individual suffering is often caused by the sin of others. So much suffering is caused by murder, adultery, theft, sexual abuse, unloving parents, reckless or drunken driving, slander, unkindness or selfishness of one kind or another. Some have estimated that perhaps as much as 95% of the world's suffering can be accounted for in this way.

This leaves a small proportion which can only be explained as being the result of the fact that we live in a fallen world: a world where all creation has been affected by the sin of human beings. It is the result of Adam and Eve's sin that 'thorns and thistles' entered the world (Genesis 3: 18). Ever since that time 'the creation was subjected to frustration' (Romans 8: 20). 'Natural' disasters are a result of this disorder in creation.

Human freedom does not always answer the question why a particular individual or nation suffers so much, but it does help explain the origin of suffering. All suffering is the result of sin, either directly as a result of my own sin, or the result of someone else's sin, or indirectly, as a result of living in a fallen world.

God works through suffering

Suffering is never a 'good' in itself, but God is able to use it for good in a number of different ways.

First, suffering is used by God to draw us to Christ.

God whispers to us in our pleasures, speaks in our conscience, but shouts in our pains; it is His megaphone to

rouse a deaf world . . . No doubt Pain as God's megaphone
is a terrible instrument; it may lead to a final and unre-
pented rebellion. But it gives the only opportunity the bad
man can have for amendment. It removes the veil; it plants
the flag of truth within the fortress of a rebel soul.[6]

This has proved true time and again in Christian
experience. We meet those who have only begun to
think about God as a result of suffering the loss of a
loved one, a broken relationship or some other pain in
their lives.

Secondly, God uses suffering to bring us to Christian
maturity. Even Jesus 'learned obedience from what he
suffered' (Hebrews 5: 8). God uses suffering to build
our characters. One image used by the New Testament
is that of the discipline of children. The writer of
Hebrews says that 'our fathers disciplined us for a little
while as they thought best; but God disciplines us for
our good, that we may share in his holiness' (Hebrews
12: 10). He points out that 'no discipline seems pleasant
at the time, but painful. Later on, however, it produces
a harvest of righteousness and peace for those who
have been trained by it' (Hebrews 12: 11).

Peter uses a completely different image: that of a
metal worker refining silver and gold. He writes that
his readers may all 'have had to suffer grief in all
kinds of trials' (1 Peter 1: 6). He goes on to explain
why God allows this: 'These have come so that your
faith – of greater worth than gold, which perishes
even though refined by fire – may be proved genuine
and may result in praise, glory and honour when
Jesus Christ is revealed' (1 Peter 1: 7).

God also uses suffering to make our lives more
fruitful. Jesus, using a different image on a similar
theme, said that as a gardener prunes the vine, so God

prunes every fruitful branch 'so that it will be even more fruitful' (John 15: 2).

This again has proved true, time and again, in Christian experience. Smith Wigglesworth, who had a remarkable ministry of healing, said: 'Great faith is the product of great fights. Great testimonies are the outcome of great tests. Great triumphs can only come after great trials.'

David Watson wrote shortly before his death:

> There is no doubt that millions of Christians all down the centuries have become more Christ-like through suffering. I know of many who have an almost ethereal beauty about them, refined through pain. In fact those who have experienced more of the love of God than anyone I have ever met have also endured more suffering. When you crush lavender, you find its full fragrance; when you squeeze an orange, you extract its sweet juice. In the same way it is often through pains and hurts that we develop the fragrance and sweetness of Jesus in our lives. An agnostic Professor of Philosophy at Princeton University became a Christian when he studied carefully the lives of some of the great saints of God throughout the history of the Church. What struck him especially was their radiance in the midst of pain. Often they suffered intensely, far more than most other people, yet through all their agony their spirits shone with a glorious lustre that defied extinction. This philosopher became convinced that some power was at work within them, and this discovery eventually brought him to Christ.[7]

A barrister, and now circuit judge, Christopher Compston wrote:

> Over twenty-three years ago, my first son Harry died

after only thirty-six hours. At the time, his death seemed monstrously unfair and, in one sense, it undoubtedly was. Now, with hindsight, I am quite certain his death was one of the best things that has ever happened to me in that it began the process of breaking me down so that, with God's grace, I could begin to understand how other people felt and how other people suffered.[8]

Our temptation would be to say to God, 'I'm quite happy as I am. Please leave me alone.' But, as C. S. Lewis points out, that would be to want God to love us less.

Over a sketch made idly to amuse a child, an artist may not take much trouble: he may be content to let it go even though it is not exactly as he meant it to be. But over the great picture of his life – the work which he loves, though in a different fashion, as intensely as a man loves a woman or a mother a child – he will take endless trouble – and would, doubtless, thereby *give* endless trouble to the picture if it were sentient. One can imagine a sentient picture, after being rubbed and scraped and re-commenced for the tenth time, wishing that it were only a thumb-nail sketch whose making was over in a minute. In the same way, it is natural for us to wish that God had designed for us a less glorious and less arduous destiny; but then we are wishing not for more love but for less.[9]

Thirdly, God often uses suffering to bring about his good purposes. Paul tells us that 'in all things God works for the good of those who love him, who have been called according to his purpose' (Romans 8: 28).

We see an example of this in the life of Joseph (Genesis 37-50). He suffered from rejection by his close family, was separated from those he loved and forcibly removed to Egypt, away from his father whom he did not see again for twenty years. In Egypt, he was unjustly imprisoned for a crime that he did not commit. For thirteen years he faced trials, temptations and testing until at the age of thirty he was made ruler over Egypt and was put in a position to save the lives of not only his family, but all of God's people. Towards the end of his life he was able to say to his brothers about his suffering: 'You intended to harm me, but God intended it for good to accomplish what is now being done, the saving of many lives' (Genesis 50: 20).

It is not always easy to see at the time what God is doing. Earlier on in his life, Joseph would not have been able to see it so clearly. Often we cannot work out what is going on or why we are suffering in the way we are.

Handley Moule, when he was Bishop of Durham, had the task of visiting the relatives of 170 miners who had been killed in a mining accident. While he was wondering what to say to them, he picked up a little bookmark his mother had given him. As he held it up, on the reverse side of the crocheted bookmark there was a tangled web. There was no rhyme, no reason, no pattern, nothing. But on the other side it said, 'God is love.' The world may seem a tangled web, but behind it all is the love of God.

We have seen that we can begin to make sense of some suffering by seeing how God uses it to bring us to Christ, to mature holiness and to work out his good purposes for our lives. Yet this still leaves some suffering which we cannot comprehend or account for in any of these ways.

God more than compensates for our suffering

We see in the story of Joseph how God blessed him in the midst of his suffering. Even as a slave to Potiphar, 'the Lord was with Joseph and he prospered . . . the Lord gave him success in everything he did' (Genesis 39: 2-3). When he was in prison again 'the Lord was with him' (Genesis 39: 21) and granted him favour in the eyes of the chief jailer so that he handed over to him the entire prison administration, 'because the Lord was with Joseph and gave him success in whatever he did' (Genesis 39: 23). God gave him such remarkable supernatural gifts that even Pharaoh recognised him as a man obviously filled with the Spirit of God (Genesis 41: 38) and put him in charge of the whole land of Egypt (v 41). In this position, he had the joy of seeing his entire family reunited and rescued from starvation.

Job went through catastrophic suffering, losing all his wealth, then all his children and finally suffering from the most horrific disease. At the end of the book we read how the Lord blessed the latter part of Job's life more than the first. As well as great wealth, Job had seven sons and three beautiful daughters. He lived to a great age and saw his children, grandchildren and great grandchildren.

For many, like Joseph and Job, the blessings of God, even in this life in and through our suffering, far outweigh the sufferings themselves. But the New Testament never leads us to assume that this will always be the case. Rather, every Christian is promised something even greater: the hope of heaven. Paul says, 'I consider that our present sufferings are not worth comparing with the glory that will be revealed in us' (Romans 8: 18), and on another occasion he wrote, 'For our light and momentary troubles are achieving for us an eternal glory that far out-weighs them all' (2 Corinthians 4: 17).

Gavin Reid, the Bishop of Maidstone, tells of a boy in his congregation, who shattered his back falling down the stairs at the age of one and had consequently been in and out of hospital. When Gavin interviewed him in church the boy remarked that 'God is fair.'

Gavin stopped him and asked, 'How old are you?'

The boy replied, 'Seventeen.'

'How many years have you spent in hospital?'

The boy answered, 'Thirteen years.'

He was asked, 'Do you think that is fair?'

He replied, 'God's got all of eternity to make it up to me.'

God has indeed all eternity to make it up to us, and the New Testament is full of promises about how wonderful heaven will be. All creation will be restored. Jesus will return to earth to establish a new heaven and a new earth (Revelation 21: 1). There will be no more crying, for there will be no more pain and suffering. We will change our frail, decaying, mortal bodies for a body like that of Jesus' glorious resurrect-ed body. We shall be reunited with all those who have died 'in Christ' and we shall spend eternity together in the presence of the Lord. As Martin Luther once said, 'I would not give one moment of heaven for all the joys and riches of the world, even if it lasted for thousands and thousands of years.'

We live in a materialistic world which has almost entirely lost the eternal perspective. We need to take a long-term view and understand the suffering of this life in the context of eternity. This is not 'pie in the sky when you die'. As the theologian Alister McGrath points out in his book on suffering, that taunt evades the question: 'Is it true?' 'If the Christian hope of heaven is an illusion, based upon lies, then it must be abandoned as misleading and deceitful. But if it is true, it must be embraced and allowed to transfigure our entire understanding of the place of suffering in life.'[10]

God is involved in our suffering

We must be prepared to acknowledge that there is no simple definitive answer to the 'Why?' of suffering. We may approach the problem from a different perspective: God is a God who suffers alongside us.

· This fourth insight is perhaps the most important of all. I once heard John Stott say, 'I could never myself believe in God, if it were not for the cross.' God is not a God who is immune from suffering. He is not looking on as an impassive observer, far removed from the suffering world. We see that throughout the Bible and, supremely, we see it in the cross. He is, in Tertullian's phrase, 'the crucified God'. God was 'in Christ', reconciling the world to himself (2 Corinthians 5: 19). He became one of us; he suffered in all the ways in which we suffer. He does not just know about suffering – he has suffered himself. He knows what we are feeling when we suffer.

In 1967, a beautiful athletic teenager named Joni Eareckson had a terrible diving accident at Chesapeake Bay which left her a quadriplegic. Gradually, after the bitterness, anger, rebellion and despair, she came to trust the sovereignty of God. She built a new life of painting (using her mouth to hold the paintbrush) and public speaking. One night, three years after the accident, she realised that Jesus empathised with her completely. It had not occurred to her before that on the cross Jesus was in a similar pain to hers, unable to move, also paralysed.[11]

The playlet, *The Long Silence*, powerfully makes the same point:

At the end of time, billions of people were scattered on a great plain before God's throne.

Most shrank back from the brilliant light before them. But some groups near the front talked heatedly – not with cringing shame, but with belligerence.

'Can God judge us? How can he know about suffering?' snapped a young brunette. She ripped open a sleeve to reveal a tattooed number from a Nazi concentration camp. 'We endured terror . . . beatings . . . torture . . . death!'

In another group a young man lowered his collar. 'What about this?' he demanded, showing an ugly rope burn. 'Lynched . . . for no crime but being black!'

In another crowd, a pregnant schoolgirl with sullen eyes. 'Why should I suffer?' she murmured. 'It wasn't my fault.'

Far out across the plain there were hundreds of such groups. Each had a complaint against God for the evil and suffering he permitted in his world. How lucky God was to live in heaven where all was sweetness and light, where there was no weeping or fear, no hunger or hatred. What did God know of all that man had been forced to endure in this world? For God leads a pretty sheltered life, they said.

So each of these groups sent forth their leader, chosen because he had suffered the most. A Jew, a young black man, a person from Hiroshima, a horribly deformed arthritic, a thalidomide child. In the centre of the plain they consulted with each other. At last they were ready to present their case. It was rather clever.

Before God could be qualified to be their judge, he must endure what they had endured. Their decision was that God should be sentenced to live on earth – as a man!

'Let him be born a Jew. Let the legitimacy of his birth be doubted. Give him a work so difficult that even his family will think him out of his mind when he tries to do it. Let him be betrayed by his closest friends. Let him face false charges, be tried by a prejudiced jury and convicted by a cowardly judge. Let him be tortured.

'At the last, let him see what it means to be terribly alone. Then let him die. Let him die so that there can be no doubt that he died. Let there be a great host of witnesses to verify it.'

As each leader announced his portion of the sentence, loud murmurs of approval went up from the throng of people assembled.

And when the last had finished pronouncing sentence, there was a long silence. No-one uttered another word. No-one moved. For suddenly all knew that God had already served his sentence.[12]

The knowledge of his suffering removes what Jürgen Moltmann has called the 'suffering in suffering'. We are not alone in our pain. When we suffer, he suffers with us.

How do we respond to suffering?

When we are suffering we will not always be able to work out why. God never told Job why he was suffering, but he told him there was a good reason. He pointed out that Job knew very little about the universe and asked him to trust God. The book of Job is not so much about why God allows suffering as it is about how we should respond to suffering.

The questions we need to ask ourselves are these:

First, 'Is this suffering a result of my own sin?' If it

is, we can ask God to reveal the specific sin. God will never leave us with a nebulous feeling of guilt. That kind of condemnation may come from Satan, but never from God. If there is a particular sin, we need to repent and ask God's forgiveness and cleansing.

Secondly, we need to ask, 'What are you saying to me through this?' There may be some particular lesson God wants to teach us.

Thirdly, we need to ask, 'What do you want me to do?'

Next, we need to hold on to our hope. This life is always a mixture of battle and blessing, and in times of battle, we need to remember that they do not last for ever and often blessing is just around the corner. Whether it is or not, we can be sure that one day we will go to be with the Lord for ever. Meanwhile, we need to keep our eyes fixed on him (Hebrews 12: 2), knowing that he is more than able to sympathise with us as he has suffered more than we ever will.

When we see others suffering, we are called to show compassion. In the face of great suffering, attempts to rationalise can be counter-productive. Even if their suffering is caused by their own sin, we are in no position to throw stones; we are all sinners, and we need to be very careful about making judgements. Not all suffering, as we have seen, is directly related to sin. Usually, the most positive thing that we can do is to put an arm around the person and 'weep with those who weep' (Romans 12: 15, RSV).

We are right to resist suffering because, as we have seen, it is an alien intrusion into God's world. Jesus fought against suffering wherever he came across it. He fed the hungry, healed the sick and raised the dead. He saw his ministry in terms of preaching good news to the poor, proclaiming freedom to the captives and recovery of sight to the blind and releasing the oppressed. We are called to follow in his steps.

Finally, and in summary, we need to come back yet again to the cross of Christ. For it is here that we begin to understand why a God of love should allow suffering. First, we see the results of human freedom: it was sin that put Jesus on the cross. We see human wickedness at its worst. We see that God was dealing with the results of man's abuse of his freedom, in paying the price for that sin.

Secondly, we see God working through suffering. Those who nailed Jesus to the cross intended it for evil; but God intended it for good – the saving of many lives.

Thirdly, we see that God more than compensates for suffering. Jesus 'who for the joy set before him endured the cross' (Hebrews 12: 2) saw ahead to his resurrection and as a result of that to our resurrection also.

Fourthly, and most important of all, we see that God himself is not removed from suffering, but suffers for us and with us.

FOR FURTHER READING

C. S. Lewis, *The Problem of Pain* (Fount).
John Stott, *The Cross of Christ* (IVP), especially chapter 13.
David Watson, *Fear No Evil* (Hodder & Stoughton, 1984).

NOTES

1. John Stott, *The Cross of Christ* (IVP, 1986), p311.
2. C. S. Lewis, *The Problem of Pain* (Fount, 1940), p14.
3. *Ibid*, p59.
4. David Watson, *Fear No Evil* (Hodder & Stoughton, 1984), pp114-115.
5. *The Times* (19th October 1991).
6. C. S. Lewis, *op cit*, pp81, 83.
7. David Watson, *op cit*, pp119-120.
8. Christopher Compston, *Recovering from Divorce* (Hodder & Stoughton, 1993), p142.
9. C. S. Lewis, *op cit*, pp30-31.
10. Alister McGrath, *Suffering* (Hodder & Stoughton, 1992), pp100-101.
11. Joni Eareckson and Joe Musser, *Joni* (Pickering & Inglis, 1976), p96.
12. John Stott, *The Cross of Christ* (IVP, 1986), pp336-337.

2
What About Other Religions?

The impression is often given that Christianity is dying out in the United Kingdom. It is said that we live in a pluralist society in which other religions are gradually taking over. Actually, this impression of a multi-faith Britain is misleading. Only 2.5% of the population are adherents of other faiths. Some 10% go to Christian churches and 80% would probably go to a Christian church if they went anywhere.

Worldwide, Christianity is by far the largest 'religion'. According to the *Encyclopedia Britannica*, it has 1,700 million adherents, amounting to 32.9% of the world population. There are 880 million Muslims, 663 million Hindus and 311 million Buddhists, in addition to many other smaller groupings such as Jews, Sikhs, Bahais and tribal religions. Atheists amount to a mere 4.5% of the world population.

Even if Christianity predominates, we still need to face the question of what Christians say about other religions. Modern communications have made us all increasingly aware of other faiths. We are brought into contact with many religions on television and radio, as well as through personal contact in the classroom, neighbourhood, work and social activities. What are we to say about these other religions?

Is Jesus the only way to God?

The answer of the New Testament is an emphatic 'Yes'.

Jesus himself said, 'I am the way and the truth and the life. No-one comes to the Father except through me' (John 14: 6). He claimed to be the way to God and, indeed, the only way. The columnist Bernard Levin makes the point that Jesus used unequivocal language:

> I take it that a religion which claims to be following the truth, the whole truth and nothing but the truth must, even if only by a process of elimination, think that the other religions are, for all their holiness and worship, mistaken. I, of all people, should not bandy scripture with experts, but in these ecumenical days it is surely reasonable to ask Christianity what its founder meant when he said, 'None shall come to the Father but by me.' I do not offer those words to give offence, but many a devout Christian is worried by them, and many a bishop, opening his heart to other faiths, must be hard put to it to provide an answer. I doubt if you will get a very convincing answer anywhere, bishop or no bishop.[1]

When Peter and John healed the crippled man outside the temple, a large crowd gathered. Peter proclaimed Jesus as the 'author of life' who had been crucified but was now resurrected and glorified. They were arrested and put on trial and asked 'by what power' the crippled man had been healed. Peter, 'filled with the Holy Spirit', replied that it was 'by the name of Jesus Christ of Nazareth' and that 'salvation is found in no-one else, for there is no other name under heaven given to men by which we must be saved' (Acts 4: 12).

Peter, inspired by the Holy Spirit, is unequivocal.

Jesus is the only name that can save. His answer is consistent with the rest of the New Testament. St Paul is equally emphatic: 'For there is one God and one mediator between God and men, the man Christ Jesus' (1 Timothy 2: 5). So the writer of Hebrews warns us that there is no other means of escape except through Jesus Christ: 'How shall we escape if we ignore such a great salvation?' (Hebrews 2: 3).

What makes Jesus unique? First, he is unique in his qualification. Peter proclaimed him as the 'Holy and Righteous One' (Acts 3: 14), the 'author of life' (v 15). He is the one the prophets foretold (v 18). He is the 'Christ' (v 20). He is the one whom the early church worshipped as God.

This sets him apart from the leaders of the other great world religions. Muslims do not like being described as Muhammadans because they do not worship Muhammad. 'No one in the Islamic world has ever dreamed of according to him divine honours – he would have been the first to reject any such suggestion as blasphemy.'[2] It is not clear whether Buddha believed in the existence of God as such. 'Early or classical Buddhism had no god.'[3]

Secondly, Jesus is unique in his achievement. As Peter asserts, 'salvation is found in no-one else, for there is no other name under heaven given to men by which we must be saved' (Acts 4: 12). We all need a saviour because we have all sinned and we cannot save ourselves from the results of sin. None of the other great religions even claims to have a saviour. 'The English Buddhist, Maurice Walsh, pointed out that the Buddhist view of Buddha is very different from the Christian view of Christ. He stressed that The Buddha is thought of as a Teacher – not as a Saviour.'[4] Likewise, Muhammad is regarded as a prophet – not as a saviour. In Islam, sinners will face judgement without forgiveness.

By contrast, Jesus is the one who brings salvation. He saves us from our guilt, he saves us from the addictive power of sin and he saves us from the judgement we all deserve.

Thirdly, Jesus is unique in his resurrection. Peter described him as the one 'whom God raised from the dead' (Acts 4: 10). The resurrection is a unique event in the history of the world.

> The Pali Canon of Buddhism records the great entrance of . . . the Buddha into Nirvana . . . but there is no suggestion that the Buddha will continue to be present with his followers after his death; the *dhamma*, the teaching, will take his place and will be their guide . . . the exact date of the death of the prophet Muhammad is known. No one has ever supposed that he survived the accident of physical death.[5]

By contrast, the resurrection of Jesus lies at the heart of the Christian faith. Jesus Christ is alive today. We can know him. We cannot know Buddha or Muhammad. Jesus, the unique Son of God, the unique Saviour, the one uniquely raised from the dead, is the only way to God. If Jesus is the only way to God, this immediately raises two further questions: first, 'What do we say about other religions?' Secondly, 'What about those who have never heard about Jesus?'

What do we say about other religions?

The fact that Jesus is the only way to God does not mean that we simply write off all other religions as misguided or demonic. Jesus said, 'I am the Truth.'

In him, ultimate truth is to be found and he is the standard by which all truth claims are to be tested. But this does not mean that parts of the truth cannot be found in other religions. Indeed, we would expect to find truth in other religions for at least three reasons.

First, although God's revelation of himself in Jesus, witnessed to in Scripture, is unique and final, God has partially revealed himself in creation. 'The heavens declare the glory of God; the skies proclaim the work of his hands' (Psalm 19: 1). The pinnacle of his creation is human life. As Sir Isaac Newton, the brilliant physicist and mathematician, said, 'In the absence of any other proof, the thumb alone would convince me of God's existence.'

Therefore, the psalmist says, only a fool can claim that 'there is no God' (Psalm 14:1; 53:1) 'For since the creation of the world God's invisible qualities – his eternal power and divine nature – have been clearly seen, being understood from what has been made, so that men are without excuse' (Romans 1: 20). From creation, it is possible for men and women to find out the truth about God's existence and gain an insight into his character: his power and his glory. The evidence provided by creation is available to all, and could therefore be found in other religions.

Secondly, human beings are made in the image of God and God has given us a conscience with which to distinguish right and wrong. As Paul put it, 'Indeed, when Gentiles, who do not have the law, do by nature things required by the law . . . they show that the requirements of the law are written on their hearts, their consciences also bearing witness, and their thoughts now accusing, now even defending them' (Romans 2: 14-15). Thus, it is not surprising that the essence of 'the golden rule' ('Do to others what you would have them do to you' – Matthew 7:12) is contained in almost every religion from Confucius (551-479 BC) onwards.

Thirdly, in every heart there is a hunger for God. God has 'set eternity in the hearts of men' (Ecclesiastes 3: 11). Deep down no one is satisfied by materialism: we know there is more to life. There is a God-shaped gap in the heart of every human being. This hunger drives us to search for God. It is one of the explanations as to why there are so few atheists in the world and why so many seek earnestly after God.

It is understandable then that we find good in many religions. Of course, we will be challenged as Christians by aspects of the lives of adherents to other religions; for example, their commitment, their devotion or their dedication to what they believe.

It also explains why there is often a certain continuity for those who become Christians from other faiths. Bishop Lesslie Newbigin, who was a bishop in South India for forty years, spoke of

an element of continuity which is confirmed in the experience of many who have become converts to Christianity from other religions. Even though this conversion involves a radical discontinuity, yet there is often the strong conviction afterwards that it was the living and true God who was dealing with them in the days of their pre-Christian wrestlings.[6]

Nevertheless, it is sheer nonsense to assert that all religions are equally true or that all religions lead to God. The theologian, Alister McGrath, points out that some world religions are avowedly non-theistic and that 'a religion can hardly lead to God if it explicitly denies the existence of a god or any gods'.[7] Equally, it is absurd to suggest that a religion which asserts that there is a god and one that asserts there is no god are both equally true. Since there are contradictions between the religions, there must be error somewhere. Indeed, we would expect to find error in other religions.

We are all fallen human beings (Christian and non-Christian alike), and none of us can find God by ourselves. But God has revealed himself in the person of Jesus – who is 'the truth'. Only in Jesus Christ do we find infallible truth. That is not to say that Christians are infallible, or that our understanding of the truth is infallible, but that God's revelation in Jesus Christ is infallible. He is the standard by which all truth claims must be examined.

By putting other religions alongside God's revelation in Jesus Christ, we see that they contain both truth and error. There is a dark side to other religions. There is, of course, a dark side to the way Christianity is being used by people, but there is no dark side to God's revelation in Jesus Christ.

This is not arrogant, narrow minded or illiberal, as some would suggest. As C. S. Lewis wrote:

If you are a Christian you do not have to believe that all the other religions are simply wrong all through. If you are an atheist you do have to believe that the main point in all the religions of the whole world is simply one huge mistake. If you are a Christian, you are free to think that all those religions, even the queerest ones, contain at least some hint of the truth. When I was an atheist I had to try to persuade myself that most of the human race have always been wrong about the question that mattered to them most; when I became a Christian I was able to take a more liberal view. But, of course, being a Christian does mean thinking that where Christianity differs from other religions, Christianity is right and they are wrong. As in arithmetic – there is only one right answer to a sum, and all other answers are wrong; but some of the wrong answers are much nearer being right than others.[8]

What about those who have never heard about Jesus?

This is the second question raised by the New Testament's claim that there is no other way to God. If we can only be saved through Jesus, are all the rest damned? If so, is that not unjust? In answering these questions I usually try to make the following five points.

First, the Bible is a practical book, not a philosophical one. It does not answer hypothetical questions directly. This question can only ever be hypothetical, since it can only be asked by someone who has heard about Jesus.

Secondly, we can be sure that God will be just. When Abraham asked the rhetorical question, 'Will not the Judge of all the earth do right?' (Genesis 18: 25), he clearly expected the answer, 'Yes, of course he will.' We need not fear that God will be unjust. He will be more just than we are; not less. On the

Judgement Day, every right-thinking person will say of God's judgement: 'That is completely just.'

Thirdly, what we do know is that no one will be saved by their religion. We are saved by God's unde-served love through faith in Jesus Christ (Ephesians 2:8). He died for us so that we can be forgiven. We receive salvation when we accept the gift by faith.

Fourthly, it is important to note that it is possible to be saved by grace, through faith, even if someone has never heard of Jesus. 'Abraham believed God, and it was credited to him as righteousness' (Romans 4: 3). Paul tells us that David also speaks of 'the blessed-ness of the man to whom God credits righteousness apart from works' (Romans 4: 6). This is possible because the cross is effective for all those who lived before as well as after Jesus. Abraham and David were forgiven because of what Jesus was to do for them on the cross. They did not have the advantage that we have of knowing how it is possible to be for-given. They did not have the assurance that we have as a result of knowing about 'Jesus Christ and him crucified' (1 Corinthians 2: 2). Nevertheless, Paul tells us that they were justified by faith.

In the same way, the person who lived at the time of Jesus or after him would be justified by faith – even if they had not heard about him. So Jesus tells us in the parable of the Pharisee and the tax collector that the tax collector who said, 'God, have mercy on me, a sinner,' went home justified before God (Luke 18: 9-14). Surely the same is true for anyone today who has not heard of Jesus but did what the tax collector did.

So the essential elements would seem to be a God-given sense of sin or need, and a self-abandonment to God's mercy. If a man of whom this is true subsequently hears and understands the gospel, then I myself believe that he would be among the company of those, whom one does sometimes meet on the mission field, who welcome and accept it at once, saying (in effect): 'This is what I have been waiting for all these years. Why didn't you come and tell me before?' And if he never hears the gospel here on earth, then I suppose that he will wake up, as it were, on the other side of the grave to worship the One in whom, without understanding it at the time, he had found the mercy of God.[9]

Fifthly, as John Stott points out, there are biblical grounds for great optimism. Abraham's descendants (spiritual as well as physical) will be 'as numerous as the stars in the sky and as the sand on the seashore' (Genesis 22: 17). 'In the same vein we seem to be assured by Paul that many more people will be saved than lost because Christ's work in causing salvation will be more successful than Adam's in causing ruin and because God's grace in bringing life will overflow "much more" than Adam's trespass in bringing death.'[10] (See Romans 5: 2.)

If that is the case, why should we bother to tell others about Jesus? First, because the glory of Jesus Christ is at stake. Secondly, because Jesus commanded us to go into all the world and tell the good news. Thirdly, because without knowing about Jesus no one could have the assurance of forgiveness and the abundant life he offers both in this life and in the life to come. For Jesus is not only the way and the truth, he is also 'the life'.

What should we do?

We have no excuse. No one who has read this chapter will ever be able to say, 'I never heard about Jesus.'

So also we have no other escape. As the writer of Hebrews warns us all, 'How shall we escape if we ignore such a great salvation?' (Hebrews 2:3).

As far as others are concerned, our task is to tell them the good news about Jesus. If the early Christians had not been willing to tell the good news about Jesus to those who already had a religion of their own, Christianity would have died in a generation.

> The Christian points to the one Lord Jesus Christ as the Lord of all men . . . the Church does not apologise for the fact that it wants all men to know Jesus Christ and to follow him. Its very calling is to proclaim the Gospel to the ends of the earth. It cannot make any restrictions in this respect. Whether people have a high, a low or a primitive religion, whether they have sublime ideals or a defective morality makes no fundamental difference in this respect. All must hear the Gospel.[11]

Of course we need to be humble and sensitive. Christians are no better than those of other religions or those of no religion. We are all in the same boat; we all need a saviour and there is no room for arrogance.

Secondly, we need to be positive. Peter in Acts 4 did not attack other faiths. He preached the good news about Jesus.

Thirdly, we need to be respectful. We need to respect everyone as those who were made in the image of God – whether they are Christians or not.

Finally, we need to be courageous. The early Christians were unashamed witnesses to Jesus. Their message was unpopular and it got them into trouble. But they did not stop. We need to do the same in an age when toleration, not truth, is the order of the day.

It is important to remember that 'the pluralism of the first and second centuries AD was the greatest in extent and intensity the world has ever seen'. But, as Michael Green goes on to say, 'Far from closing our options, pluralism allows us to proclaim an undiluted gospel in the public square and in the supermarket of faiths, allowing others the same right. Let the truth prevail and let craven silence be banished.'[12]

FOR FURTHER READING

Stephen Neill, *The Supremacy of Jesus* (Hodder & Stoughton, 1984).
Lesslie Newbigin, *The Gospel in a Pluralist Society* (SPCK, 1989).
John Stott, *The Contemporary Christian* (IVP, 1992), chapter 18.

NOTES

1. Bernard Levin, *The Times* (27th January 1992).
2. Stephen Neill, *The Supremacy of Jesus* (Hodder & Stoughton, 1984), p82.
3. John Stott, *The Contemporary Christian* (IVP, 1992), p308.

4. John Young, *The Case Against Christ* (Hodder & Stoughton, 1986), p152.
5. Stephen Neill, *op cit*, p82.
6. Lesslie Newbigin, *The Finality of Christ* (John Knox Press, 1969), p59.
7. Alister McGrath, *Bridgebuilding* (IVP, 1992), p151.
8. C. S. Lewis, *Mere Christianity* (Fount, 1952), p39.
9. J. N. D. Anderson, *Christianity and Comparative Religion* (IVP, 1970), p105.
10. John Stott, *op cit*, p319.
11. Lesslie Newbigin, *op cit*, p59.
12. Michael Green, *Evangelism through the Local Church* (Hodder & Stoughton, 1990) p75.

3

Is there Anything Wrong with Sex Before Marriage?

In the second half of the twentieth century a major sexual revolution has taken place. Our society has been saturated with sexual stimulation in films, television, advertising and glossy magazines. No longer is it only the top shelf in newsagents which is devoted to sex; now the middle-shelf magazines tell you 'everything you wanted to know about sex, plus much much more'. Sex has become the idol of our times.

At the same time, another alarming revolution has taken place: marriage and family life is breaking down. A century ago the divorce rate was 200 per annum. By 1987 it had risen to 151,000 per annum – a three-fold increase since 1967. Almost one half of marriages now end in divorce. The financial cost of broken marriages, based on hard statistics such as legal aid and supplementary benefits, is a staggering £2 billion per year.[1] More important, the human cost is incalculable.

So we see in our society an increasing unwillingness to enter marriage in the first place. More and more couples live together without getting married. Only two in three conceptions now occur inside marriage and lead to birth. John Diamond, writing in his Private Life column in *The Times*, says, 'Nowadays, for most people at least, marriage is one of those optional things you do if you want to make a particular sort of statement about the life you already share.'[2]   There seems to be something fundamentally wrong with the so-called sexual liberation of the twentieth century.

On the other hand, there have been times when the church and society have had a totally repressive and negative attitude towards sex.   Origen, one of the early theologians of the church, regarded sex as something inherently sinful: 'Adam did not have sexual knowledge of his wife until after The Fall. If it had not been for The Fall, the human race would likely have been propagated in some very mysterious or angelic manner without sex and, therefore, sin.'

In the Middle Ages, Yves of Chartres taught that complete abstinence from sexual relationships had to be maintained on five out of seven days a week: on Thursdays in memory of the arrest of our Lord, on Fridays in honour of his death, on Saturdays in honour of the Virgin Mary, on Sundays in commemoration of the Resurrection, and on Mondays out of respect for the faithful departed!

The Victorian era is also well-known for its sexual prudery when some even considered that the legs of pianos had to be covered! These prejudices and the sense of guilt associated with sex still affect the lives of many.

Both the obsession of the modern era and the repression of former times are a far cry from the biblical understanding, which is not outdated but highly relevant to us and our society today. Indeed, it is here that we find the Maker's instructions which bring liberation and fulfilment.

God, in his love, has given us a good plan

The Bible affirms our sexuality; God made us 'male and female' (Genesis 1: 27). The body is good; we are 'fearfully and wonderfully made' (Psalm 139: 14). Jesus had a physical body. Everything God made was good – including our sexual organs which he designed for our enjoyment. The sexual urge is God-given and, like fire in the fireplace, is a great blessing when enjoyed in the right context. In God's original creation Adam and Eve were 'both naked, and they felt no shame' (Genesis 2: 25). There was no guilt attached to their sexuality, which is why we should be able to talk openly and frankly about these matters without embarrassment. As C. S. Lewis points out, 'Pleasure is God's idea, not the Devil's.' God is not looking down from heaven and saying, 'Goodness gracious, whatever will they get up to next?'

Further, the Bible celebrates sexual intimacy as a profound form of communication. 'Adam knew Eve his wife, and she conceived and bore Cain' (Genesis 4: 1, RSV). In the Song of Solomon we see the delight, tenderness, contentment and satisfaction that can be derived from sexual intimacy. The tone is set in the opening verses: 'Let him kiss me with the kisses of his mouth – for your love is more delightful than wine' (Song of Songs 1: 2).

Sex in its right context is good and beautiful. God has a high view of sexual relationships. Marriage is a reflection of Christ's relationship with the church (Ephesians 5) and there can be nothing higher than that. That is why Christian married couples should be encouraged to delight in one another and enjoy sexual intimacy to the full. There is great freedom within marriage; sex should never become mundane or boring. This contrasts sharply with the attitude of many so-called defenders of sexual liberation. Marcelle d'Argy Smith, editor of *Cosmopolitan*, said recently, 'Sex is like Big Ben. I'm glad it's there and if I were less tired I could go and have a look at it.'[3]

The biblical context of sexual intercourse is the life-long commitment in marriage between one man and one woman. When Jesus spoke of marriage he went back to the creation account: 'For this reason a man will leave his father and mother and be united to his wife, and they will become one flesh' (Matthew 19: 5-6 quoting Genesis 2: 24). Here we see the key to the biblical understanding of marriage. First, there is a leaving – a public act of lifelong exclusive commitment. Secondly, there is a uniting of the man and the woman. They are 'glued together' in marriage. Thirdly, it is in this context that the 'one flesh' sexual union takes place. It is not just physical and biological, but emotional, psychological, spiritual and social. Our whole beings are united in marriage, and sexual intercourse is not just a physical response to a physical desire. The physical union both expresses the other unions and also brings them about. We express ourselves with our bodies and the act of intercourse expresses our unity.

God has so designed our bodies and our sexuality that we can go on exploring and enjoying one another for a lifetime. An actor, well-known for his romantic roles, was asked on a TV programme, 'What makes a great lover?' He answered: 'A great lover is someone who can satisfy one woman all her life long; and who can be satisfied by one woman all his life long. A great lover is not someone who goes from woman to woman. Any dog could do that.' Of course, this applies to men and women alike.

Next, in God's order, partnership and procreation are linked. God blessed Adam and Eve and said to them, 'Be fruitful and increase in number' (Genesis 1: 28). God so designed our bodies that the same act of intercourse should have the effect of both uniting us in partnership and being the means by which procreation takes place. This does not mean that every act of intercourse should have that intention, but it is part of God's design that it takes a man and a woman to have a baby. God's ideal is that every child should be conceived in an act that expresses love and commitment and that they should grow up in that atmosphere. The most important relationship for a child's security is the one between the two parents.

God, in his love, warns against human distortions

Tragically, God's plan has been distorted by human sin. Our sin affects every area of our human lives, including our sexuality. 'All have sinned and fall short of the glory of God' (Romans 3: 23). Obviously, not everyone's sexuality is equally distorted, and some will retain the original creation order more than others, but none of us is in a position to pass judgement. When Jesus said to those about to stone the woman caught in adultery: 'If any one of you is without sin, let him be the first to throw a stone at her' (John 8: 7), the context was not just any sin, but specifically sexual sin.

The fact that we are all guilty does not mean that it does not matter, or that we should make no attempt to avoid sin. Jesus told the woman, 'Leave your life of sin' (John 8: 11). The Maker's instructions were given out of love. It is not that when he sees people enjoying themselves he says, 'I'll soon put a stop to that!' but rather that God does not want us to get hurt.

As we have seen, God designed sexual intercourse for our enjoyment in the context of marriage. Any sex outside marriage is a distortion of God's good gift and falls short of his ideal. Jesus took the Bible as his authority and if Jesus is our Lord we must follow his example. This does not mean we condemn the people involved, for we are called to accept and love people unconditionally. At the same time, we must speak out against the sin. Indeed, it is part of loving people.

Any sexual intercourse outside marriage is forbidden. Adultery is specifically outlawed by the seventh commandment, and when we see the betrayal of trust and the wreckage of families stemming from this deceit we are able to understand why. However, sex before marriage is certainly widely defended and needs more discussion.

Because sexual intercourse is a life-uniting act, Paul says that even if a man has sex with a prostitute he becomes 'one with her in body' (1 Corinthians 6: 16). He commands his readers to 'flee from sexual immorality' (v 18). The word he uses includes all sex outside marriage. It is the same word that Jesus used in Mark 7: 21 and Paul used elsewhere (1 Thessalonians 4: 3-8).

Most would agree that sex and love should go together. Promiscuity, although common practice today, has few serious defenders, but most people would defend the practice of sex before marriage in a more stable relationship. The teaching of Jesus in the rest of the New Testament is against such a practice, for it is not just love and sex that must go together but sex and long-term commitment to each other in marriage. Such commitment is evidenced in our society by the marriage vows. Marriage is not just a piece of paper, nor is the wedding day simply for dressing-up and getting together with family and friends. It is a public and responsible expression of lifelong commitment, and the certificate of marriage is a public document accessible to all. In this context, sexual intercourse signifies, seals and brings about an unbreakable, total personal unity. Without such a commitment, sex is cheapened, being 'a life-uniting act without a life-uniting intent'.[4] The life-uniting intent is evidenced by marriage alone; engagement is not sufficient, for engagements can always be broken (this is part of the point of a period of engagement). Irrevocable commitment comes only with the public act of marriage.

This is God's pattern for sexual relationships. Sex

outside marriage may feel good. However, when God's pattern is broken people get hurt.

First, we risk hurting ourselves. When a relationship involving sexual intercourse breaks down, someone always gets hurt and usually it is both parties who suffer. This is true of divorce, but it is also true of sexual relationships between unmarried people, leaving both parties scarred. God is not a spoil-sport. Rather, he does not want us to get hurt. Furthermore, the marriage itself is far more likely to work. Pre-marital sex increases the chances of extra-marital sex and, of course, adultery is one of the leading factors in marriage breakdown. Recent figures have indicated that the divorce rate is far lower among those who have waited until their wedding day. For example, according to recent research, of couples who married for the first time in the 1980s, those who pre-maritally cohabited were 60% more likely to have divorced after eight years of marriage than similar couples who had not done so.[5]

If we keep to God's laws, we live under his blessing, and part of that blessing will be the blessing of the wedding day. Even those who are not Christians often recognise that they have lost something by living together before the marriage. John Diamond, writing in *The Times* about those who have waited until their wedding day, says they

> have something to look forward to. They leave their parents' home on the morning of the wedding as children and climb into bed that night as adults. There is so much to play with, and all at the same time: the new house, the giggling joint washing-up sessions, the bed, the joint cheque book – and because it all started with the wedding, it all becomes part of the same adventure.

The rest of us, the over-the-broomstick lot, get up, tap our partners on the shoulder, make jokey gulping noises, get a mini-cab round to the register office, listen to our mates making faux-ironic jokes about what we will be getting up to tonight, ho-ho, and then come back and do last night's washing-up. We try out the new Mr and Mrs names for a day or two, then realise that our joint cheque book and the mortgage deeds are in the old names anyway, and go back to them.

We've done cheque books a dozen times and deciding on the new paint for the hall a hundred. There is nothing new you can tell us about the socks-on-the-bathroom-floor conundrum; and whose-turn-is-it-for-Waitrose mantra is one that we already know by heart. While newly met newlyweds can set sail on their magical voyage of discovery, our own marital plans mean we are stuck on the Woolwich ferry arguing about who forgot to bring the packed lunch.[6]

If the two parties involved do eventually marry each other, they often regret that they did not wait until their wedding day. One man who regretted that he had not waited said to me that it had been like opening the Christmas presents before Christmas day.

Secondly, we risk hurting others. If the relationship does not last, there may be a damaging effect on a future marriage. Previous sexual relationships can lead to jealousy and a lack of a feeling of being `special' for the marriage partner. Indeed, it can make marriage itself less likely. In our society this especially affects women who have had a number of sexual relationships. Men perversely get away with being regarded as 'studs'. Women are sometimes regarded as 'used goods' with little left to give to a marriage relationship. The hurt involved can be very serious.

If there is an unwanted pregnancy, then hard decisions have to be made. There are a number of possibilities: abortion, bringing up the child in a single-parent family, adoption, a 'shot gun' wedding or an illegitimate child. All of these involve hurt for different reasons, and all fall short of God's ideal for both the parties involved and the child. Those of us in pastoral ministry see the agony that results every time this happens.

Thirdly, we risk hurting society. The family unit is one of the basic building blocks of society. Increasingly, it is recognised that sex outside marriage can be a factor that leads to family breakdown. In turn, family breakdown is one of the reasons for the soaring crime rate. In fact, both are symptoms of a society which has turned away from God's standards. Immanuel Jakobovits, Chief Rabbi from 1967-1991, writing about marital infidelity, said that 'the cost to society is incalculable: above all in terms of the millions of children now being raised in a moral wasteland, without the shelter of a loving home. Is it any wonder that from their number countless embittered, selfish, lonely and sometimes violent citizens are recruited to swell the ranks of the anti-social?'[7]

Our bodies were not designed for sex outside marriage. Before AIDS it was unhealthy; now it can be fatal. For too long the glossy magazines fooled us that 'free love' is free. But there is a price to be paid. If we had kept to God's standards, AIDS would not have spread. The best way to stop it now is to return to God's standards.

Fourthly, we hurt God. The most important consideration of all is that breaking God's laws has serious consequences: it cuts us off from him. That is why it is impossible to hold together a wholehearted love and service of God and disobedience in the area of sexual morality. It is this which stops many today giving their lives to Christ, and they lose out on abundant and eternal life for something which in the long run only does them harm. Others are torn apart by the tension in their lives between a supposed profession of faith and a life which they know goes against such a profession.

The New Testament warns us that God will judge all sin, including immorality (1 Thessalonians 4: 6). God's laws are there to protect us and to protect society – given out of love. But there are serious consequences when we break his laws.

God, in his love, sent Jesus to restore us

God's standards are very high and in our society they are not easy to keep. However, God has not left us alone and he came to set us free. He did not come to condemn the world but to save it, giving us the power to resist temptation, and to bring forgiveness and healing.

How to resist

It is possible to stop having sexual intercourse, even though it may be very difficult. When someone comes to Christ, they may be sleeping with a partner who is not a Christian and it may be hard to explain to that person why they will not sleep with them any more, and this involves rejection and hurt. Yet it is almost impossible to make any real progress in the Christian faith until such a sexual relationship ends, because we cannot hold on to sin and be wholehearted in our Christian lives at the same time. If both parties come to Christ at the same time, it is easier, but it still requires great self-control. I have seen several couples who have succeeded in this area and have found enrichment from God in their relationship. Usually they have married later and found God's blessing also in their family life. Some think they will lose the respect of their friends, but the opposite is often the case. If we live by these standards we will have an opportunity to influence society, rather than being squeezed into the world's mould.

Many fear that there will be a gap in their lives if they stop making love, and that they will not be as close to their partner. This is not the case unless sex is the sole basis for the relationship; in which case it is better that the relationship ends because it does not have a solid foundation. Indeed, this is one of the dangers of sex before marriage: it clouds our judgement about the rightness of the relationship. It is much easier to work out whether we are suited to be partners for life if our judgement is unclouded by a sexual relationship. As one twenty-seven-year-old woman put it: 'Once the sex had been taken away, I realised there was nothing left.' If the relationship is right, there will not be such a gap; rather there will be a depth of understanding, respect, trust and dignity.

There may even be a sense of relief. Another woman said, 'I felt as though a huge weight, which I hadn't realised was there, lifted off my shoulders.' Sexual intercourse is not the only way to demonstrate love. In fact, self-control often shows more love and sets a good pattern for married life when, from time to time, self-control needs to be exercised. If the relationship is conducted along these lines it makes it easier for both parties to decide whether or not it is right to get married.

How do we avoid getting into such a situation in

the first place? Jesus began with the heart, the eyes and the thoughts. He said, 'Anyone who looks at a woman lustfully has already committed adultery with her in his heart' (Matthew 5: 28). This is where self-control begins for us all. All of us will be tempted to have immoral thoughts – Jesus was tempted also – but temptation is not sin. It is not the thoughts that are sinful; rather it is the entertaining of them. The more we give in, the more difficult it gets. The more we resist, the easier it gets. James, the brother of Jesus, wrote, 'Resist the devil, and he will flee from you. Come near to God and he will come near to you' (James 4: 7-8). It tends to be a spiral, either going up or down.

We need to help one another by not putting temptation in the way. For example, it is not a good idea to sleep in the same bed if you are trying to resist temptation. Single people sometimes ask, 'How far can we go?' The Bible does not lay down the rules and nor should we. People and circumstances vary. We need to remember that it is always hard not to go further next time. No married couple I know ever regretted going too slowly before they were married.

If all this leads then to great sexual frustration, is masturbation a way out? This can be a taboo subject, especially among Christian people. In fact, nearly all adolescents and many adults do masturbate. It is estimated that 95% of men and over 50% of women have some experience of masturbation. Of course, it is not physically harmful and it is nowhere specifically condemned in the Bible.

However, there are three concerns. First, it has a tendency to become obsessive. Secondly, it depersonalises sex – our sexuality was intended to move us towards personal communion. Thirdly, it is often associated with lustful thoughts. But the guilt usually associated with masturbation is out of all proportion to its seriousness. Martin Luther describes it as 'a puppy sin'. One pastor said it was like 'biting our nails' – something many do as part of growing up. It is not a good idea, but should not be taken too seriously unless it becomes excessive.

In all these areas, we need to avoid the guilt and condemnation spiral which can bring us down and lead us to further sin. The Spirit of God sets us free where a set of rules would be powerless (Romans 8: 1-4). Jesus' provision of the Holy Spirit means that it is possible to break free.

Forgiveness

As we have seen earlier, all of us have failed in this area to a greater or lesser extent. None of us is in a position to throw stones at anyone else. Jesus died for us so that we could be forgiven. The way to receive forgiveness is through repentance. In Psalm 51 we see a model for repentance following sexual sin. This is the psalm attributed to David after he had committed adultery with Bathsheba. The remedy for sin is not to make excuses or to do things to make up for it. Rather it is confession and repentance. However far we have fallen, we can make a new start in Christ.

I love the story Jackie Pullinger tells of a seventy-two-year-old woman in her church who was a heroin addict and a prostitute for sixty years. She used to sit outside a brothel waiting for customers, poking the sewers with a stick so that they would flow more freely. She was being injected in her back three times a day because there were no more veins in her arms and legs. She had no identity card and did not even exist as far as the Hong Kong government was concerned. She was 'one of those who are not'. Seven years ago she gave her life to Jesus Christ and received forgiveness for her sins. She went to live in one of Jackie's houses and God started to heal her. In the summer of 1992, she married Little Wa who was aged seventy-five. Jackie described it as 'the wedding of the decade'. The former prostitute was able to walk down the aisle in white, cleansed and forgiven by Jesus Christ.

Jesus enables us both to receive forgiveness and to give it. Many have been sinned against in this area. Some say that one person in ten has been sexually abused, and often people go through life crippled by these experiences. Freedom always begins with forgiveness – receiving God's forgiveness and then, in gratitude for his forgiveness, forgiving those who have sinned against us.

Conclusion

The heart of our sexuality is not the biological dimension but the personal one. Jesus himself points the way to a state beyond marriage. In heaven there will be no marriage. Here on this earth, as John Stott, himself unmarried, writes,

> it is possible for human sexual energy to be redirected (`sublimated' would be the Freudian word) both into affectionate relationships with friends of both sexes and into the loving service of others. Multitudes of Christian singles, both men and women, can testify to this. Alongside a natural loneliness, accompanied sometimes by acute pain, we can find joyful self-fulfilment in the self-giving service of God and other people.[8]

Sex is not an ultimate goal. Our society, as we have seen at the beginning, has made an idol out of sex. Sex has replaced God as the object of worship. We need to reverse this. If we seek pleasure as a god, in the long run we find emptiness, disappointment and addiction. If we seek God, we find, among other things, ecstatic pleasure.

FOR FURTHER READING

Lewis Smedes, *Sex for Christians* (Triangle SPCK, 1993).
Richard Foster, *Money, Sex and Power* (Hodder & Stoughton, 1985).
John White, *Eros Defiled* (IVP, 1977).

NOTES

1.   Statistics from *The Times* (31st May 1989).
2.   *The Times* (21st May 1992).
3.   *Daily Mail* (9th February 1993).
4.   Lewis Smedes, *Sex for Christians* (Triangle, SPCK, 1993), p130.
5.   John Haskey. Pre-marital cohabitation and the probability of divorce: analyses using new data from the General Household Survey. *Population Trends* 68 (HMSO Publications), quoted in *The Times* (19th June 1992).
6.   *The Times* (25th June 1992).
7.   *The Times* (22nd September 1993).
8.   John Stott, *The Message of the Thessalonians* (IVP, 1991), pp84-85.

4
How Does the New Age Movement Relate to Christianity?

The New Age movement is based on an astrological theory that each star age lasts for 2,000 years. It is claimed that we are moving from the age of Pisces to the age of Aquarius. The age of Pisces lasted 2,000 years. The word 'Pisces' means fish – the symbol of Christianity. Now we are moving, we are told, to the age of Aquarius, symbolised by a rainbow. The watershed is around the year 2,000.

But the New Age is already dawning. In the memorable words of the musical *Hair* which hit London in the 1960s and is currently being revived:

When the moon is in the seventh house, and Jupiter
aligns with Mars,
Then peace will guide the planets, and love will steer the
stars.
This is the dawning of the Age of Aquarius!
Harmony and understanding, sympathy and trust
abounding,
No more falsehoods or derision, golden living dreams of
visions,
Mystic crystal revelation, and the mind's true liberation.
Aquarius! Aquarius! Aquarius!

The age of Pisces was the age of Yang, the masculine.

The age of Aquarius will be the age of Yin, the feminine. The age of Pisces was the age of the assertive and the rational. The age of Aquarius will be the age of the intuitive and the spiritual. New Agers believe that this scientific, materialistic, mechanistic era is coming to an end and humanity is progressing into a time of greater spirituality and world harmony. In some ways it is part of as profound and all-encompassing a movement as the European Renaissance 500 years ago.

We in the Western world live in extraordinary and changing times. We are living in the midst of a revolution in the way we think and the way in which we look at the world. The Enlightenment worldview and framework is collapsing around us.

In pre-Enlightenment times, reason was viewed as a tool of understanding but subordinated to the revealed truth of Christianity which was seen as thoroughly supernatural. The seventeenth and eighteenth centuries saw a shift in the European way of thinking. Central to Enlightenment thought were the use and celebration of reason – the power by which we understand the universe and improve our condition. The Enlightenment brought enormous progress in science, technology and medicine, but within it were the seeds of its own destruction. Revelation was made subject to reason. Although the Enlightenment was for the few, nineteenth-century secularisation was for the many. Yet, in spite of all the changes of atmosphere, the Victorians preserved a society which was powerfully influenced by Christian ideas and continued to accept the Christian ethic as the highest known to mankind. It was not until the twentieth century that the full implications and the fruit of the seeds sown were seen in a devastatingly clear light.

Now, in our own day, many are questioning the suppositions of the Enlightenment. We can no longer be described as a secular society – we live in an age which is the most religious for several generations. It is an age of religious pluralism. Rising up out of this shift of thinking, the New Age movement rejects rationalism. It has highlighted well the emptiness and shortcomings of rationalism and materialism. It emphasises experience and values spirituality, but it goes further than this.

What is the New Age movement?

Graham Cray, Principal of Ridley Hall Theological College in Cambridge, has described our culture as a 'pick-and-mix culture' and the New Age movement as a classic first attempt at a new worldview. The New Age movement is an umbrella term that covers various diverse and disparate movements with a seemingly limitless array of disconnected beliefs and lifestyles. It is almost impossible to define because it has so many different branches. It has no leader, no organisation, no structure and no headquarters. It is a ground-swell, an uncentralised movement of many diverse constituents. The most that can be said is that a New Ager is someone who looks at reality in a certain way and reacts in a certain way. Caryl Matrisciana, looking back on her experience of many years involved in the New Age, describes it as being like the recipe for a cake:

2 cups of hope (carefully sift out all fear)
2 cups of altered consciousness (Yoga, drugs, or meditation to taste)
3 tablespoons each of self-awareness, self-improvement and self-esteem (be sure to melt away anything negative)
1 heaped teaspoon of peace
1 large dollop of love
1 generous pinch each of humanism, Eastern mysticism and occultism
1 handful of holism
1 scoop of mystical experience.

Mix thoroughly together. Bake in a warm, friendly environment. Fill with your most appealing dreams. Garnish generously with positive thoughts and good vibrations.[1]

It is a mixture of Eastern mysticism and occult practices which have been given a Western materialistic flavour. On the surface, parts are either good or harmless. It often comes in the guise of self-improvement programmes, holistic health, a concern for world peace, ecology and spiritual enlightenment. Indeed, by themselves, certain elements of the New Age, such as the stress on good nutrition, the avoidance of drugs and respect for creation, find an ally in Christianity. However, often under the sugar coating there is a dangerous pill. As St Paul warns us, 'Satan himself masquerades as an angel of light' (2 Corinthians 11: 14).

First, many of the New Age teachings are derived from Eastern mysticism. Hindu and Buddhist doctrines have been adapted for the Western world. A string of gurus have blended Eastern concepts with a Western thirst for fulfilment, expression and enlightenment. There is a great deal of teaching on TM (transcendental meditation), reincarnation, karma, Zen, yoga and levitation.

Secondly, there is the influence of nature religions from around the world, including Druidism, the folk beliefs of American Indians and Wicca witchcraft.

Thirdly, there are a number of practices in the movement which are overtly occult. Astrology, horoscopes, fortune-telling, clairvoyance, consulting the dead, spiritism, mediums, channelling, spirit guides and tarot cards are all widely used in the movement. All practices such as these are condemned in the Bible: 'Let no-one be found among you who sacrifices his son or daughter in the fire, who practises divination or sorcery, interprets omens, engages in witchcraft, or casts spells, or who is a medium or spiritist or who consults the dead. Anyone who does these things is detestable to the Lord . . .' (Deuteronomy 18: 10). These warnings are reiterated elsewhere in the Bible (Leviticus 19: 26, 31; Galatians 5: 20; Revelation 9: 20-21).

The influence of the movement is enormous. One survey reckoned that 25% of Americans are involved in some form of New Age practice. It even penetrated to the heart of the White House, with former First Lady Nancy Reagan consulting astrologists for guidance. In Germany it is estimated that there are half a million involved in the New Age. In France there are 40,000 professional astrologists. In the UK it is fast affecting every area of our culture, with even members of the Royal Family visiting New Age healers. In the 1992 General Election, the Natural Law Party, which advocated TM and 'yogic flying', raised enough support to run for election in most constituencies in the country.

It has infiltrated the arts and music world. For example, Boy George's band 'Jesus Loves You' sings 'Bow down to Hari Krishna'. He is reported as saying:

> I think of myself as being God-conscious but I don't necessarily have a defined image of what God is. I feel I'm a free spirit and the fact that Jesus existed is neither here nor there . . . God to me is total, unconditional love. I have Sufi, Christian, Buddhist friends and I respect what they believe in, and in their temples I bow down. I believe there's a force out there that matches us step for step. I'm not explaining it brilliantly but it's a feeling for me.[2]

Terence Trent D'Arby has asserted that the late Marvin Gaye is dictating songs to him from heaven – he is what the New Agers call a 'channel'.[3]

Bookshops nearly all have large New Age sections. The clairvoyant, medium and spiritual healer Betty Shine's books, *Mind to Mind* (published in 1989) and *Mind Magic* (in 1991), became instant bestsellers, lasting a combined total of nineteen weeks in the *Sunday Times* Top Ten list.

International capitalism is also affected. A growing number of companies encourage TM and training courses based on New Age concepts. Some finance houses employ astrologers and use other New Age techniques to increase productivity. In the medical profession New Age techniques are creeping in. One survey found that 700 doctors in England practise TM and recommend it to their patients. Alternative medicine, which sometimes involves New Age practice, is becoming increasingly fashionable.

Young people are growing up in an environment which is influenced by the movement. Cinemas and videos show overtly occult films and also those which have a subtle New Age tinge. Computer games are often full of references to magic and occult themes. Many of the toys and games like 'Dungeons and Dragons' and TV programmes like *The Crystal Maze* have a New Age flavour. It is even affecting our schools. *The Times* reported on a school in Lancashire where TM is taught – modelled on similar schools in the USA. Children aged ten and upwards begin the day by shutting their eyes and reciting their mantras. Pictures of the Maharishi Mahash Yogi are on the wall. TM is part of a whole new system of learning known as 'United Field Education System'. One New Ager, John Dunphy, wrote that he was convinced that 'the battle for humankind's future must be waged and won in the . . . school classroom by teachers who correctly perceive their role as the proselytizers of a new faith . . . The classroom must and will become an arena of conflict between the old and the new – the rotting corpse of Christianity . . . and the new faith of Humanism'.[4]

Even the church is not immune. One church in Central London allows its premises to be used for seminars and talks which expressly advocate New Age practices such as shamanism, planetary healing and chakra dance.

What are the beliefs of the New Age movement?

The New Age movement is so disparate that it is hard to summarise its beliefs. John Stott describes them in what he calls 'three pithy sayings': 'All is God', 'All is one' and 'All is well'.[5]

The first, 'All is God', is generally known as pantheism. God is in everything. He is depersonified. He is an impersonal energy, a creative force. A godlike force runs through all creation – trees, animals, rocks and people. In many strands of New Age thinking, there is no distinction between the creator and what he has created. The earth is divine, as are the stars and planets. This leads to a return to the pagan worship of Mother Earth and to the belief that the stars and planets and even crystals have power and influence.

In the New Age movement, there is no God outside his creation. God lies within each of us, and we are each a part of God, or as Shirley Maclaine, a prominent New Age advocate, puts it, 'Everyone is God. Everyone.' The way to find God is to look within. Hence the title of one of her books is *Going Within*. Swami Muktananda says, 'Kneel to your own self. Honour and worship your own being. God dwells within you as you.' It is exactly as G. K. Chesterton described in 1908 in his book *Orthodoxy*: 'Of all conceivable forms of enlightenment the worst is what . . . people call the inner-light. Of all horrible religions the most horrible is the god within. That Jones shall worship the God within him turns out ultimately to mean that Jones shall worship Jones.' Mankind has fallen once again for the primeval temptation 'you will be like God' (Genesis 3: 5).

Although there is a great deal of talk about compassion and love, the movement is very self-centred. The starting point for change (with perhaps the long-term goal of helping others) is the development of the self. The worship of self manifests itself in books and courses on self-realisation, self-fulfilment, self-help, self-confidence, self-improvement, self-worth, self-esteem and self-love. The highest goal is to find one's own happiness, satisfaction and success. To find one's own self is to find God.

This, of course, is an explicit assault on the self-denial at the heart of true Christianity. It is the opposite of the New Testament where the way of fulfilment is loving and serving a personal God and loving and serving others. The way of fulfilment is not self-worship but self-denial, exemplified supremely in the life, death and resurrection of Jesus Christ.

Secondly, 'All is one' – for which the technical term is 'monism'. The New Age is essentially syncretistic. It attempts to reconcile opposites and bring about a synthesis of all religions. In so doing, it rejects much orthodox Christianity which is seen as rigid, structured and blinkered.

The movement rejects moral absolutes; 'sin' is not a

popular word in the New Age. Our problem is not sin, but ignorance of our true self and potential. This is solved by enlightenment, spiritual revelation and education. For some, there is no objective standard of right and wrong. As one spiritual sage from India put it, when speaking to Caryl Matrisciana, 'It's not a question of whether you are good or bad . . . good and bad are relative. They are two sides of one coin, part of the same whole.'[6]

In a similar vein, Carl Frederick wrote: 'You are the supreme being . . . there isn't any right or wrong' (*Playing the Game the New Way*). Shirley Maclaine's philosophy, along with many other New Agers, could be summed up as: 'If it feels good, do it.' The New Age offers the attraction of a spirituality without the cost of repentance. It is sometimes called 'hippy values for a yuppie lifestyle'.

Guidance comes from within. Hence many advocate abortion, homosexuality and promiscuity. Ryan and Travis in the *Wellness Work Book* write:

So if love is as natural as breathing, and eating, and working and playing, it is as natural as 'sexing'. Besides, if love becomes our 'life support system' then every decision we make, sex included, will be guided by it. We will choose to have sex with one another if it enhances our experience of unification with all that is.

Since our problem is not sin but ignorance, there can be no judgement (again, an unpopular word in the New Age). In contrast to the Christian view that 'man is destined to die once, and after that to face judgment' (Hebrews 9: 27), reincarnation is taught almost universally throughout the movement. It is not always taught as cosmic justice, where we will be graded up or down depending on how good or bad we have been. Rather, everyone is eventually making progress onwards and upwards towards complete spiritual enlightenment and perfection. Again, they have fallen for Satan's lie – 'You will not surely die' (Genesis 3:4).

Monism ('All is one') is taken to even further extremes in some parts of the New Age, in which there is no distinction made between God and Satan. Since all is one, some end up worshipping the devil. Lucifer himself is actually worshipped in some strands of the movement.

The third saying with which John Stott summarises New Age belief is 'All is well'. There is an optimism which runs through it all. We are making evolutionary progress towards Utopia. Many believe we will see the establishment of a new world order and a new world religion. Some even believe there will also be a new world government, and that this new Utopia will be ushered in by a world teacher who will bring economic and religious unity.

On Saturday, 24th April 1982 full-page advertisements appeared in major national newspapers around the world headed 'The Christ is now here'. Underneath it read:

As Christians await the second coming, so the Jews await the Messiah, the Buddhists the fifth Buddha, the Muslims the Imam Mahdi, and the Hindus await Krishna. These are all names for one individual. His presence in the world guarantees there will be no Third World War . . . He has not as yet declared his true status, and his location is known only to a very few disciples. One of these has announced that soon the Christ will acknowledge his identity and within the next two months will speak to humanity through a world wide television and radio broadcast. His message will be heard inwardly, telepathically, by all people in their own language. From that time, with his help, we will build a new world.

The person behind it all turned out to be a man called Benjamin Crane, and over a decade later the promises have not been fulfilled.

Jesus warned against such claims:

For false Christs and false prophets will appear and perform great signs and miracles to deceive even the elect – if that were possible. See, I have told you ahead of time. So if anyone tells you, 'There he is, out in the desert,' do not go out; or, 'Here he is, in the inner rooms,' do not believe it. For as lightning that comes from the east is visible even in the west, so will be the coming of the Son of Man (Matthew 24: 24-27).

What is wrong with the New Age movement?

The New Age movement is right to challenge the prevailing materialism and rationalism. It is right to emphasise the importance of experience and to value spirituality. It is right to stress compassion, love and unity. Millions in the movement are on the right track in the sense that they are searching for spiritual reality. Yet these emphases fall way short of the glorious truths of Christianity.

We in the church are often to blame for having presented a form of Christianity that is hierarchical, structured and narrow-minded. We can sympathise with David Icke when he wrote, 'I feel the traditional Church as an organisation has let down the world badly with its dogma and rigidity.'[7]

The remedy lies not in the rejection of Christianity, but in a reappraisal of what is at the heart of the Christian faith. When we look at this, we see how far short the New Age movement falls of the glorious truth about the trinitarian God of the orthodox Christian faith.

First, it does not get near the truth about God the Father. God is not an impersonal, abstract force, but he is the transcendent personal creator of the universe. And yet he is immanent. He wants to be in a relationship with us as human beings. We can speak to him and he speaks to us. He is a Father who loves us and we are called to respond in love to him and for our brothers and sisters. These are the glorious truths on which our Christian culture is built. The New Age movement will take us back to paganism, and St Paul warns us against those who 'exchanged the truth of God for a lie, and worshipped and served created things rather than the Creator' (Romans 1: 25).

We were made to live in a relationship which involves the love and worship of God. As St Augustine put it, 'You have made us for yourself, and our heart is restless until it rests in you.' That is why there is a restlessness within the New Age movement. There is a continual searching for an illusory peace. Shirley Maclaine writes: 'Whenever I ask people what they want for themselves and for the world, the answer is almost always the same – peace.'[8] Yet she has clearly not found it herself. After each new experience she speaks of a wonderful peace and she sleeps 'like she has not done for years', and yet soon she is searching again for some new experience because the 'peace' is short term and illusory.

One woman in our congregation who was involved in the New Age for about three years told me about her initial feeling of self-growth, and being set to 'break the rules'. But soon she found she was imprisoned.

> I was like a lamb to the slaughter. It was like being on drugs. I was constantly looking for bigger experiences. I went on more and more expensive courses. I felt I was going out of my mind. It leaves you stuck in a place you don't understand – where you can't relate to the world. It led me away from anything good and nourishing. You just don't know when you are going to be healed.

She eventually found fulfilment, peace and healing in a relationship with God the Father, who alone can bring true and lasting peace.

Secondly, the New Age does not get near the truth about God the Son. Jesus is seen as one of the ascended masters, along with Buddha, Krishna and others. Extraordinary rewritings of the New Testament gospel accounts abound. In her book *Going Within* Shirley Maclaine claims that Jesus was a member of the Essenes whose 'teachings, principles, values and priorities in life were so similar to those of the so-called New Age today . . . Christ demonstrated what we would today call precognition . . : levitation, telepathy and occult healing'.[9]

David Icke claims that between the age of twelve and thirty 'Jesus travelled widely to countries like India, Greece, Turkey, Egypt, France and England . . . He once had to self-heal himself after contracting tuberculosis.' According to Icke, his disciples were 'all Planetary Devas'. After his death on the cross 'friends buried the body in a cellar and it has never been found'.[10] Needless to say, there is not a shred of historical evidence to support either Shirley Maclaine's or David Icke's absurd speculations.

At the most extreme end, the Bhagwan Shree Rajneesh bought a town in America and set up his own Ashram where his Western disciples underwent enlightenment therapy, which put emphasis on sex, drugs and violence. The net gain to the Bhagwan was a garage full of ninety-three Rolls Royces. Jesus was rich, but for our sakes became poor so that we might become rich. The Bhagwan was poor, but became rich and in doing so left a lot of others very poor.

In trying to accommodate Jesus into New Age thinking, they miss out on the glorious truth of Jesus Christ, that he is 'the way and the truth and the life' (John 14: 6). He was, and is, God made man for our salvation. In his great love, Jesus died on the cross for us, in order to free us from guilt, addiction, fear and death. He made forgiveness possible, bringing us friendship with God, the experience of his love and the power to change. Consequently, he liberates us to love and serve others and to become more like Jesus himself. These things are at the heart of the biblical understanding of salvation. This salvation is not something we could ever earn or achieve ourselves; it is a free gift from God. The only salvation in the New Age is self-salvation and the only forgiveness is self-forgiveness. In *A Course in Miracles*,[11] a typical workbook used by many in the movement for daily reading, lesson 70 is headed 'My salvation comes from me'. The reader is urged to repeat, 'My salvation comes from me. It cannot come from anywhere else.' On the contrary, the New Testament asserts that Jesus is the only way of salvation (Acts 4: 12). The New Age misses out on this wonderful news.

They miss out too on the good news of his resurrection. Michael Green writes:

Our destiny is not to go through many purgative reincarnations until the grossness of our lives is melted away, but after death to share in the resurrection life of which the Easter Jesus is the pledge. 'To depart is to be with Christ, which is far better.'

'We shall be like him, when we see him as he is.' That is the conviction of those who knew him. Is it beyond belief? Not reincarnation, based on *karma*, but resurrection, based on the cross and resurrection of Jesus, which points both to our forgiveness and to our destiny. A totally different world view. And one which challenges us to make up our minds, and choose.[12]

Thirdly, the New Age does not get near the truth about God the Holy Spirit. In the New Age we see a search for spiritual power, spiritual experience and transformed lives. There is no greater spiritual power than the power of the Holy Spirit; no greater experience than the fullness of the Holy Spirit and no more effective power to transform our lives. New Age transformation is sought through altered consciousness, yoga, TM, visualisation, the seven chakras, rebirthing, or astral travel. There is a power in these things, but it does not compare to the power of the Holy Spirit. Indeed, even if it begins quite innocently, involvement in some New Age practices can sometimes lead to opening oneself to evil powers which seek to control rather than to liberate.

One woman told me how she had tried Buddhism, Zen, Hinduism, TM, the occult, and all kinds of other New Age practices. Then one day she read Jackie Pullinger's book about her work among drug addicts in Hong Kong. She went out there and saw people being set free and healed by the power of the Holy Spirit. She saw the life, love, joy and peace the Holy

Spirit brought to people's lives. I asked her what the difference was between that and her experiences in the New Age. She replied that she had seen real power in both, but added, 'One power, the New Age power, meant opting out of society, whereas the power of the Holy Spirit meant opting back into society and changing people's lives.'

It is interesting that at a time of great outpouring of the power and gifts of the Holy Spirit in the church (which began at the turn of the century) we are seeing what appears to be a satanic counterfeit (which began shortly afterwards). What Satan cannot counterfeit is holiness. The Holy Spirit transforms Christians into the likeness of Jesus Christ (2 Corinthians 3: 18). The fruit of the Spirit is love, joy, peace, patience, kindness, goodness, faithfulness, gentleness and self-control (Galatians 5: 22-23).

What are we to do?

First, there is a need for a double repentance. On the one hand, if we have been involved in any way in New Age practices, whether unwittingly or not, we need to recognise that they are wrong and to ask God's forgiveness and turn away from all such things. We need to turn to Jesus Christ who died on the cross so that we could be forgiven. We need to ask the Holy Spirit to come and live within us. On the other hand, those of us who have been involved in the church need to repent of our rigidity, rationalism and failure to make the church relevant to the culture in which we live. We should also acknowledge where New Age thinking has properly challenged our own prejudices. The interest in holistic medicine, for example, does in some senses move us back towards a true Christian understanding of the human being as one – rather than a being with a sharp division between body and soul.

Secondly, we need to soak ourselves in the truth. Paul warns us: 'See to it that no-one takes you captive through hollow and deceptive philosophy' (Colossians 2: 8) and again in Timothy:

> For the time will come when men will not put up with sound doctrine. Instead, to suit their own desires, they will gather around them a great number of teachers to say what their itching ears want to hear. They will turn their ears away from the truth and turn aside to myths. But you, keep your head in all situations (2 Timothy 4: 3-5).

We don't need to read all the New Age books. The way to spot a counterfeit is to know the real thing really well. Caryl Matrisciana uses a helpful analogy:

> 'Mum's been working at the bank for over a year,' my friend Chris told me. 'And she's been getting the most *amazing* education.'
>
> 'What do you mean?'
>
> 'She's learning all about money.'
>
> 'I guess she'd have to know about money if she's going to work in a bank!' I laughed.
>
> Chris smiled. 'I mean she's *really* learning about money. They are teaching her to know the colour of each bill, the size of it, even the way it's water marked. They are showing her the details of the inks and papers.'
>
> 'How do they teach her?'
>
> 'Well, they just keep having her handle it. They point out all the various things they want her to remember. But they figure the more she works with money, feels it,

counts it, and stacks it, the more familiar it'll be to her.'

'That makes sense, I suppose. But what's the point?'

'Here's the point. Yesterday they blindfolded her. They slipped a couple of counterfeit bills in her stack of money. She picked them out by touch!'

'So she's studying counterfeit money too, then?'

'No . . . that's just it. The people at the bank know that a person doesn't need to study the counterfeits.'

'I see. But it seems as if they're going to a lot of trouble, doesn't it?'

'Not really. The banks know that the counterfeits are getting better and better, more and more sophisticated. And it's been proved a thousand times over that *if a bank teller knows the real money extremely well, he can't be fooled by the counterfeits.*'[13]

Thirdly, we need to bring the good news of Jesus to those who are involved in the New Age. On the whole, those involved are simply people searching for the truth. They recognise that materialism does not satisfy. They recognise the limits of reason. They are seeking an experience of the spiritual. We need to demonstrate by our lives the supernatural power of God: Father, Son and Holy Spirit.

FOR FURTHER READING

Caryl Matrisciana, *Gods of the New Age* (Marshall Pickering, 1985).
Michael Green, *The Dawn of the New Age* (Darton, Longman & Todd Ltd, 1993).

NOTES

1. Caryl Matrisciana, *Gods of the New Age* (Marshall Pickering, 1985), p15.
2. Boy George, *The Independent* (Tuesday, 15th September 1992).
3. Steve Turner, *The Times* (6th July 1990).
4. Quoted in Caryl Matrisciana, *Gods of the New Age* (Marshall Pickering, 1985), p171.
5. John Stott, 'Conflicting Gospels', *CEN* (8th December 1989), p6.
6. Caryl Matrisciana, *op cit*, p81.
7. David Icke, *The Truth Vibrations* (The Aquarian Press, Harper Collins, 1991) p20.
8. Shirley Maclaine, *Going Within* (Bantam Press, 1989), p30.
9. *Ibid*, pp180-181.
10. David Icke, *op cit*, pp115-117.
11. *A Course in Miracles* (Penguin, 1975).
12. Michael Green, *The Dawn of the New Age* (Darton, Longman & Todd Ltd, 1993), p86.
13. Caryl Matrisciana, *op cit*, p220.

5
What Is the Christian Attitude to Homosexuality?

The Bible is the story of God's love to all humanity. God loves all people, irrespective of race, colour, background or sexual orientation. As we approach this subject, I am conscious of the agony that exists for many people in this area. Jesus came not to condemn us, but to save (John 3: 17). In the same way, the Christian community needs to show sensitivity and understanding towards those for whom their homosexual orientation is a daily struggle, and to affirm them as human beings loved by God.

A homosexually-orientated person is someone whose sexual preference is for someone of the same sex. Alfred C. Kinsey, in his 1948 survey of white US males, 'Sexual Behaviour in the Human Male', found that 4% were exclusively homosexual, 10% had been homosexual for up to three years and 37% had some kind of homosexual experience between adolescence and old age. This produced a popular view that approximately one in ten of the population was homosexual. However, a national survey on sexual behaviour and AIDS in Britain published by HMSO in 1993 found that only 6% of the male respondents had had a sexual experience with another man. Only 3.6% had had anal intercourse with another man. Of the

last group, two thirds had also had sexual intercourse
with a woman.[1]   The incidence of homosexual activity among women is even more rare.

These results conform with a new study of male
sexual behaviour – the most thorough carried out in
the United States since the Kinsey report. This survey
by the Alan Guttmacher Institute showed that only
1% of American men considered themselves exclusively homosexual, although 2% said they had
engaged in homosexual activity at one time or another. This contrasts sharply with the popular concep-
tion that homosexual activity is quite common.
Nevertheless, the issue affects enough people for the
question of a Christian attitude to homosexuality to
be raised frequently.

Historically, homosexually-orientated people have
often been subject to 'oppression, resentment, hostili-
ty and ridicule'.[2] AIDS is seen by some as homosexuals getting their 'just deserts'. On the other hand, the
gay liberation movement outside and within the
Christian church 'urge the view that homosexuality is
simply a natural variant of human sexuality – as natural as red hair or left-handedness – to be affirmed
and rejoiced in, and that its expression in fully loving
physical sexual embrace is well within the purpose
and will of God'.[3]

Is there a right Christian attitude towards homosexuality? Is homosexual practice an option for the
Christian? Is AIDS the judgement of God on homosexual practice? Can homosexual orientation be
changed, and is such a change desirable? What
should our attitude be to those with a homosexual
orientation? These are the questions which are
often raised and which I will try to address in
this chapter.

Is homosexual practice an option for a Christian?

In Chapter 3 we looked at the biblical view of sexual intercourse. We saw that God designed sex for our enjoyment and that the biblical view of sexual intercourse is a very positive and liberating one. We saw also that God's context for sexual intercourse is life-long commitment (in marriage) between one man and one woman (Genesis 2: 24). He did not design our bodies for homosexual intercourse. This view of marriage and sex, which Jesus quoted and endorsed, rules out all sex outside marriage, whether heterosexual or homosexual.

There are not many references to homosexual practice in the Bible, but those that are to be found are all negative. Twice in the Old Testament law the practice of homosexuality is condemned as 'detestable' (Leviticus 18: 22; 20: 13). One of the sins for which Sodom was destroyed was homosexual practice. The men of Sodom ordered Lot to bring out his two male guests, 'so that we can have sex with them' (Genesis 19: 5). Although Sodom was guilty of many other sins, the immediate context of the Lord's anger with his people was homosexual practice. In a similar way, the desire of the men of Gibeah for homosexual activity is portrayed as 'disgraceful' (Judges 19: 23).

In the New Testament, homosexual practice is among the list of things which Paul condemns. His teaching is quite explicit: 'Do you not know that the wicked will not inherit the kingdom of God? Do not be deceived: Neither the sexually immoral nor idolaters nor adulterers nor male prostitutes nor homosexual offenders nor thieves nor the greedy nor drunkards nor slanderers nor swindlers will inherit the kingdom of God' (1 Corinthians 6: 9-10).

The word translated as 'male prostitutes' refers not to prostitutes alone, but generally to the passive partners in homosexual intercourse. The word translated as 'homosexual offenders' refers to the active partners and is the word used again in the list of 'lawbreakers and rebels, the ungodly and sinful, the unholy and irreligious' (1 Timothy 1: 9). Paul assumed that homosexual practice would have been abandoned at conversion (1 Corinthians 6: 11).

In Paul's view, homosexual practice is one of the results of God taking the brakes off society as a result of man's rebellion against God. God gives us the freedom to follow our own devices, if we so choose.

> Therefore God gave them over in the sinful desires of their hearts to sexual impurity for the degrading of their bodies with one another. They exchanged the truth of God for a lie, and worshipped and served created things rather than the Creator – who is for ever praised. Amen. Because of this, God gave them over to shameful lusts. Even their women exchanged natural relations for unnatural ones. In the same way the men also abandoned natural relations with women and were inflamed with lust for one another. Men committed indecent acts with other men, and received in themselves the due penalty for their perversion (Romans 1: 24-27).

Paul is referring back again to the created order and the way in which we are designed. Homosexual practice is not 'natural'; it goes against God's created order. Paul also expressly condemns the attitude of those who 'not only continue to do these very things but also approve of those who practise them' (Romans 1: 32). Such is the defiant attitude of some of the leaders of the gay movement today that they are on dangerous ground, according to the New Testament. 'Taken together St Paul's writings repudiate homosexual behaviour as a vice of the Gentiles in Romans, as a bar to the Kingdom in Corinthians, and as an offence to be repudiated by the moral law in 1 Timothy.'[4]

It is vital to note that nowhere does the Bible condemn homosexual orientation, homosexual feelings or homosexual temptation. Temptation is not sin. Jesus was 'tempted in every way, just as we are – yet was without sin' (Hebrews 4: 15). What the Bible condemns is not homosexual preference, but homosexual practice (a distinction we will consider later in this chapter). Jesus took the Scriptures as his authority and if Jesus is our Lord, then we must follow him.

Is AIDS the judgement of God on homosexual practice?

From time to time we read in the papers of some famous person, who has either just admitted he has HIV, the AIDS virus, or who has just died of AIDS. In November 1991 Freddie Mercury, the lead singer in the rock group Queen, died of AIDS. More recently Rudolf Nureyev, the ballet dancer, died of AIDS. Kenny Everett, the entertainer, who has been openly homosexual for many years, confessed recently that he is HIV positive. A few days afterwards Holly Johnson, lead singer with Frankie Goes to Hollywood (whose hit 'Relax' urges gays to take pride in their sexuality) said he too has HIV.

AIDS is one of the biggest health threats to mankind this century and consequently has brought the issue into sharp focus. The World Health

Organisation estimates that 11-12 million are infected with the HIV virus worldwide – 1 in 250 of the world's population. By the year 2000 it is estimated that 40 million will be infected. In Africa more people may already be dying from AIDS than from famine. Worldwide, 90% of all new infections are caused through heterosexual transmission. However, in the UK heterosexual infection is still relatively small, although growing. Statistically, AIDS is still correlated to homosexual practice. Over three quarters of those who have died from AIDS probably acquired the virus as a result of homosexual intercourse. There is still, therefore, a strong link between homosexuality and AIDS in popular thinking in this country.

Obviously there is nothing in the Bible about AIDS, but we can look at the biblical principles and seek to apply them to a modern disease. We have seen that God, in his great love, has given us boundaries in order to protect us. When we cross those boundaries we often get hurt, just as when one puts a finger in the fire it gets burned. He also imposes a penalty for breaking his laws. Older theologians made a distinction between these two different types of judgement: first the judgement of God, which is the inevitable results of sin, is the *effectus* of God's judgement. Secondly, there is God's personal (though never malicious or, in a bad sense, emotional) reaction against sin known as the *affectus* of his judgement.

Let me explain this distinction by using a human analogy. There is a law against drinking and driving, the purpose of which is to protect road users from getting hurt. I read in a newspaper of a man who drove after he had drunk excessively. He crashed the car and was seriously injured; his best friend, who was a passenger, was killed. A prosecution was brought and he was sent to prison. His injuries and the death of his friend were an *effectus* of breaking the law, while the penalty of the court was an *affectus*.

How are we to see AIDS in the light of this analogy? Is it an *effectus* or an *affectus* of God's judgement? Is it like the injuries the man received, or is it like the punishment of the court?

One day God will judge the world. There will be a penalty to be paid for all sin (the *affectus* of his judgement) – in the same way that the courts punish crimes now. The judgement will be perfectly fair and just. We will either pay the penalty ourselves or, if we have put our trust in Jesus Christ, we will be saved through what he achieved for us on the cross. This is the final judgement which will occur when Jesus returns. In the meantime, God sometimes intervenes to judge now in this life – as in the case of Sodom and Gomorrah (Genesis 19) and Ananias and Sapphira (Acts 5). These supernatural acts of intervening judgement are comparatively rare throughout the Bible.

On the other hand, his judgement in the sense of *effectus* (the inevitable results of sin) is going on all the time. People are getting hurt as a result of God's laws being broken. As in the case of the drunk driver, it is not only the perpetrator of the offence who gets hurt, but there are also 'innocent' casualties like the driver's best friend.

Returning to the question of AIDS, I do not believe that it can be seen as the judgement of God in the sense of an *affectus* – his personal reaction against sin – any more than lung cancer can be seen as his judgement on cigarette smoking. Certainly, it could not be a judgement, in this sense, on homosexuality. As we have seen, 90% of the new infections worldwide are heterosexual, while female homosexuals are in the safest group. It cannot even be seen as a judgement, in that sense, against promiscuity or sex outside marriage, since some are infected through blood transfusions and others inherit it from their parents.

However, it can be seen as the *effectus* of his judgement: the inevitable results of breaking his law. In our analogy, it is the equivalent of the car crash in which both the guilty and the innocent friend were hurt. God's rules were given to protect people from getting hurt. When his laws are broken, it is often not only the law-breaker who is hurt. Sometimes the innocent are hurt also, while others get away with it entirely. Not every drunk driver crashes; not every promiscuous person contracts AIDS or other sexual diseases. Although sooner or later, the drunk driver is likely to have an accident and sooner or later homosexual activity and promiscuity are likely to lead to hurt. This is due to the way we are made and designed to live, rather than something explosively visited upon us. Just as crockery which is not dishwasher proof may crack if it is put in the machine, we were not designed for homosexual or promiscuous activity. These activities exceed our physical, emotional and spiritual tolerances and are likely to cause damage in all these areas in the long run. Homosexuality and promiscuity were unhealthy before AIDS. Now they can be fatal. As we saw in Chapter 3, if we had kept to biblical standards, AIDS would not have spread. The best way to stop it now would be to return to biblical standards.

But AIDS itself is not the real crisis in our society; rather, it is a symptom of the real crisis, which is that men and women have turned their backs on God, and we are seeing the results (Romans 1: 21).

Can sexual orientation be changed?

All our hopes are based on the cross of Christ. What the New Testament promises to repentant Christians here and now is forgiveness for the past. There is a distinction between the repentant believer who occasionally sins and the unrepentant following of a steady, unresisted course of planned disobedience. To the man or woman who repents and seeks to obey Christ, the New Testament promises total forgiveness through the cross of Christ. Homosexual practice is not the worst sin; nor is it unforgiveable.

Further, for every Christian the power of sin has been broken at the cross. Writing to the Corinthians, Paul says of the 'sexually immoral', 'adulterers', 'male prostitutes' and 'homosexual offenders': 'That is what some of you were. But you were washed, you were sanctified, you were justified in the name of the Lord Jesus Christ and by the Spirit of our God' (1 Corinthians 6: 9-11).

By using the past tense, Paul is suggesting that his readers have changed. They have given up their former practices, although some will continue to be tempted in this area all the way through their lives. God's promise is that 'no temptation has seized you except what is common to man. And God is faithful; he will not let you be tempted beyond what you can bear. But when you are tempted, he will also provide a way out so that you can stand up under it' (1 Corinthians 10: 13).

Tony Campolo writes:

It is *very* important that all of us distinguish between homosexual *orientation* and homosexual *behaviour*. Homosexual orientation is an inclination to desire sexual intimacy with members of the same sex. Homosexual behaviour is 'making love' or seeking sexual gratification through physical interaction with members of the same sex. The first is desire. The second is action. The first is temptation. The second is yielding to temptation.

I personally know many Christians with a homosexual orientation who fight against their desire for homosexual behaviour through the power of the Holy Spirit. The desire to have sexual gratification through physical involvement with persons of their own sex is a constant one (just as heterosexual desire can be a constant for many) with many of them, but they are 'more than conquerors through Christ who strengtheneth' them (Romans 8:37).

I cannot help but admire these brave saints who endure lives of sexual frustration because of their commitment to what they believe are biblical admonitions against homosexual intercourse. Many such Christians have told me about their long nights of spiritual agony as they have struggled against the flesh to remain faithful to what they believe to be the will of God. Any who believe that these homosexuals who remain celibate for the sake of Christ are anything less than glorious victors in God's kingdom ought to be ashamed of themselves.[5]

But is it possible for our sexual orientation to be changed? This is related to the discussion about what causes homosexual orientation. There are many hypotheses as to the causes, but no absolute conclusions. Some people believe that homosexual orientation is innate or inborn, although science has searched in vain to find a physical basis for homosexuality. In spite of some recent claims, there is no conclusive scientific evidence that genetic or hormonal factors are causative in homosexual behaviour. However, there is a great deal of evidence that homosexual orientation is something that is often acquired or learned. It may be caused by a number of factors: lack of love and affirmation from a same-sex parent; a dominant, controlling or overprotective and possessive mother; a weak, ineffective or rejecting father; incest or sexual abuse. All these are possible causes.

Whatever the causes, in most cases homosexually-orientated people are the product of forces over which they have little or no control, certainly in the early stages. Whether the basis is biological or sociological, it is almost certainly not their fault. We should never condemn anyone for being homosexually orientated. On the other hand, whatever the cause, everyone still has the responsibility to live with their orientation and regulate its expression. Even if there is a scientific basis, it does not mean that it is God's will. As we have seen, it is not part of the original created order, but is an indirect result of sin entering the world. Therefore, as far as possible, we should seek restoration and healing.

When the Lord returns, our bodies will be made perfect (Romans 8: 23), and all who are in Christ will be totally healed. For some, healing takes place now in this life. A 1955 British Medical Association survey listed fourteen case histories of homosexually-orientated people who were totally released after Christian conversion, and concluded: 'Homosexuals can be so changed through conversion that their sexual desire loses its mastery.'[6]

Others have been changed through the supernatural power of the Spirit or a gradual process of inner healing, which usually involves forgiving and receiving forgiveness for past hurts. For others, healing takes place through the Christian community as they develop relationships within the body of Christ and find affirmation, love and acceptance. Yet others have been helped through psychiatrists or psychologists (some working in this field have sometimes used morally dubious means to alter the orientation, and the end does not justify the means). There is no conflict between prayer and therapy, for there is only one source of all healing. The only question is whether God uses miraculous, or more ordinary, means.

The older a person is, the harder it is to change. Like any behavioural pattern, the more it is followed, the more it will become fixed. The psychiatrist, John White, writes: 'Once I experience physical pleasure with a member of my own sex, I am more likely to want to experience it again. The more frequently I experience it, the more fixed will the pattern become. What I do determines what I am, just as much as what I am determines what I do.'[7]

Although changes in orientation are more unusual, even where a pattern is apparently fixed there are some remarkable healings. I remember seeing a programme about a man called Frank who had been an active homosexual for twelve years. He could see no way out. The moment he was converted, he knew he would never be a homosexual again. Likewise, a woman called Kathy, who all her life had believed she was gay, was totally set free when Christ came into her life. At the time of the programme they had been married to each other for seven years, had six lovely children and were engaged in ministry to others with similar struggles.

Five years ago, I met a charming French violinist in his mid-twenties, who was having an affair with a man ten years older. A member of our congregation gave the man a copy of a Christian book and prayed with him that Jesus would reveal himself within twenty-four hours. That evening he and his partner were having supper when he disintegrated in tears, went into his bedroom and there had an extraordinary vision of Jesus. He gave his life to Christ. Next day, I interviewed him in church and asked him what he was going to do about the relationship. He said that he was going to end it. In order to break the news gently he went out and bought a bunch of flowers, the heads of which were closed. He prayed that by the time they were opened, his partner would have become a Christian. His partner had seen the remarkable changes in his friend and went to see the person with whom he had prayed. They too prayed, and the older man became a Christian. He also had an amazing vision of Jesus – 'the most powerful experience of my life'. He said afterwards, 'For the first time, I really knew love.' Both these men are still active Christians. The man in his mid-thirties I know well: he is now a fine Christian leader and often prays with others who are in a similar predicament to the one he was in.

I asked him recently about his experience of praying with homosexually-orientated people. He said that in his experience, lack of affirmation by a father was usually an important factor in their homosexuality. He found that homosexual relationships never quite worked and never totally fulfilled, and so consisted of two unaffirmed people looking for affirmation, while being unable to affirm each other because of their own lack of affirmation. Homosexual practice was a sexual way of receiving affirmation.

Hence, there is great power in receiving forgiveness, and forgiving fathers who have been unable to affirm their sons. Forgiveness brings freedom from the pain of that relationship and the ability to receive affirmation from our heavenly Father. He spoke of the dramatic and healing understanding which came when he had done that. He still needed to sort issues through, but the process of healing of the heart had begun: 'Healing is not an act of repression, but the way into freedom,' he said. 'The inevitable outcome is sexual wholeness – wholeness in all relationships. Homosexuals often define themselves by their sexuality – "I am my sexuality." Knowing the freedom in Christ, we cease to define ourselves by our sexuality and see sex in terms of relationships and not relationships in terms of sex.'

What should our attitude be to those involved in a homosexual lifestyle?

Although all of us were created in the image of God, we are all fallen human beings, ie, none of us is without sin. We saw in the chapter on sex before marriage that every area of our lives is affected by sin. We are all sexual sinners. None of us is in a position to throw stones at others, although the church sadly has a bad history of it. Jesus said to those about to stone a woman guilty of sexual sin, 'If any one of you is without sin, let him be the first to throw a stone at her' (John 8:7).

Jesus, who was the one person there in a position to throw stones since he was without sin, did not. Rather, he showed her great love and compassion. But he also said to her, 'Go now and leave your life of sin' (John 8: 11). Our calling is to follow Christ's example, which is to love and accept people unconditionally. At the same time, we must recognise sin as sin, rather than condoning it.

This is a unique combination. Generally the attitude towards homosexuality tends to fall into one of two opposite extremes. On the one hand, there are those who condemn those involved and are personally hostile. This attitude is along the lines of: 'Shoot the lot of them.' On the other hand, there are those who, in accepting the people, *condone* the sin. They say there is nothing wrong with homosexual practice.

We are called to love those living a homosexual lifestyle. But love does not involve condoning sin. Indeed, the opposite is the case. If we see a child about to run across a road and shout, 'Don't!', it is not because we want to ruin their fun. We warn them because we love them and we don't want them to get hurt. In the same way, we are called to speak out, when appropriate, against the practice of homosexuality. It is wrong to promote a homosexual lifestyle in schools. It is wrong to ordain unrepentant practising homosexuals into Christian leadership.

On the other hand, we are called to love people and welcome them with open arms into the church. As John Stott writes, 'At the heart of the homosexual condition is a deep loneliness, the natural human hunger for mutual love, a search for identity, and a longing for completeness. If homosexual people cannot find these things in the local "church family", we have no business to go on using that expression.'[8]

We need to promote a safe environment where the homosexually orientated can find somebody with whom they can talk and pray. Many have never been able to tell anyone about their internal battles. The ability to talk to someone about their difficulty is often the first step to bringing light into the darkness.

Further, the church should be at the forefront of bringing hope and healing to those with AIDS and HIV. A fine example is ACET (AIDS Care Education and Training), which seeks to minister to those in our society with AIDS by providing practical help in a non-judgemental way. They encourage those with HIV/AIDS to think positively about their future and educate young people in order to prevent them from becoming infected.

Love is the key from first to last. It was God who, in his love, gave us sex. In his love, he also gave us boundaries. His heart must break when he sees the mess we have got ourselves into. In his love he sent Jesus to bring us forgiveness and the power to resist temptation and also to bring healing. We are called to be like him and to go out and love as he loved us.

FOR FURTHER READING

John Stott, *Issues Facing Christians Today* (Marshall Pickering, 1984), chapter 16.
Martin Hallett, *I Am Learning to Love* (Marshall Pickering, 1987).
Leanne Payne, *The Healing of the Homosexual* (Crossway, 1984).

NOTES

1. E. G. Knox, C. MacArthur, K. J. Simons, 'Sexual Behaviour and AIDS in Britain' (HMSO), p84.
2. David Atkinson, *Pastoral Ethics in Practice* (Monarch, 1989), p73.
3. *Ibid*, p74.
4. Peter Coleman, quoted by David Atkinson, *op cit*, pp76-77.
5. Tony Campolo, *20 Hot Potatoes Christians Are Afraid to Touch* (Word Publishing, 1988), p110.
6. *Homosexuality and Prostitution* (BMA, 1955), p92.
7. John White, *Eros Defiled* (IVP, 1978), p111.
8. John Stott, *Issues Facing Christians Today* (Marshall Pickering, 1984), p321.

6
Is there a Conflict between Science and Christianity?

The theory portrayed by the mass media, for whom any confrontation is news, is that science and Christian belief are in direct conflict. There are two main reasons for this.

First, there have been times in the history of Christianity when the church has opposed the results of scientific study. Galileo, the seventeenth-century Italian astronomer, found himself in conflict with the Roman Catholic Church over his discovery that planets revolve around the sun. He was tried by the inquisition in Rome, ordered to recant and spent the final eight years of his life under house arrest.

Persecution of scientists did not end in the seventeenth century. As late as 1925, John T. Scopes, a high-school teacher from Drayton, Tennessee, was prosecuted for violating the state law by teaching the theory of evolution. He was convicted and fined $100. On appeal, he was acquitted on the technicality that he had been fined excessively.

Secondly, it is thought by many that modern scientific study explains everything that was once explained by belief in God, so that such belief is therefore now redundant. Further, it is argued that the assured results of modern science are in direct conflict with the teaching of the Bible. Some would say, for example, that modern science shows that miracles do not happen, whereas the Bible is full of miracles. Others claim that the scientific theory of the gradual evolution of humans and their organisms by natural processes is inconsistent with the account of creation in Genesis 1. The English biologist and agnostic philosopher, T. H. Huxley (1825-1895), for example, said, 'The doctrine of Evolution, if consistently accepted, makes it impossible to believe the Bible.'

In this chapter I want to look at how science and Christian belief relate to each other and, in particular, whether there is a conflict between 'the assured results of modern science' and the Christian faith.

Science and Christian faith are not incompatible

It was the Christian worldview that provided the right environment for modern science to emerge. First, the Christian faith is monotheistic. Belief in one God led people to expect a uniformity in nature, with the underlying laws of nature remaining the same in time and space. A universe that was capricious and irregular would not be capable of systematic study.

Secondly, the Christian doctrine of creation by a rational God of order led scientists to expect a world which was both ordered and intelligible. Sixteenth-century scientists reasoned that the universe must be orderly and worthy of investigation because it was the work of an intelligent creator. 'Men became scientific because they expected Law in Nature, and they expected Law in Nature because they believed in a Legislator.'[1]

Thirdly, the Christian belief in a transcendant God, separate from nature, meant that experimentation was justified. This would not have been the case under belief systems which regarded forms of matter as gods. Nor would it have been wise to experiment if you believed, as some did, that matter was essentially evil. The Christian worldview was that matter was good, but not God. So the Christian doctrine of creation 'provided an essential matrix for the coming into being of the scientific enterprise'.[2]

That Christian belief provided fertile soil for scientific experimentation is recognised by scientists, historians and philosophers. Dr Peter Hodgson, lecturer in nuclear physics at Oxford University, said, 'Christianity provided just those beliefs that are essential for science, and the whole moral climate that encouraged its growth.'[3] The historian Herbert Butterfield stated that 'science is a child of Christian thought'. The philosopher John MacMurray put it like this: 'Science is the legitimate child of a great religious movement, and its genealogy goes back to Jesus.'[4]

It is a well-established fact that for much of history Christianity and scientific study have been allies and not opponents.

Nicolaus Copernicus (1473-1543) laid the foundations of modern astronomy and the scientific revolution by suggesting, on mathematical grounds, that the earth travelled around the sun. He held office in the Polish Church as a Canon of Frauenburg Cathedral and described God as 'the Best and Most Orderly Workman of all'.

Mathematician, physicist and astronomer Galileo Galilei (1564-1642) was the founder of modern mechanics and experimental physics. He argued that the earth was not the centre of the universe. Although he was persecuted by the church, he was a devout Catholic Christian and once said, 'There are two big books, the book of nature and the book of supernature, the Bible.'

The founder of modern optics was the brilliant early astronomer and mathematician Johannes Kepler (1571-1630), best known for his discovery of the three principles of planetary motion. He was a deeply sincere Lutheran and said that he was 'thinking God's thoughts after Him'.

Perhaps the greatest scientist of all time was Sir Isaac Newton (1642-1727). He was certainly one of the most towering scientific intellects in history. He is well-known for his formulation for the laws of gravity. He was also an expert in the field of optics, astronomy, differential calculus and responsible for the first correct analysis of white light. He believed in the inspiration of Scripture and wrote theological as well as scientific books, regarding his theological books as more important. He believed that no sciences were better attested than the religion of the Bible.

Michael Faraday (1791-1867), who appears on the back of our £20 notes, was one of the greatest scientists of the nineteenth century. He discovered the phenomenon of electro-magnetic induction. He was the first to produce an electric current from a magnetic field. He invented the first electric motor and dynamo. Again, the Christian faith was the single most important influence upon him.

The same is true of many other pioneering scientists. Robert Boyle gave his name to 'Boyle's Law'; Joseph Lister pioneered antiseptic surgery; Louis Pasteur originated pasteurisation; Gregor Mendel helped form the basis for the science of genetics; Lord Kelvin was a leading light in the foundation of modern physics; James Maxwell formulated electro-magnetic theory. All these leading scientists were Christians.

Professor James Simpson, who paved the way for painless surgery through anaesthetics, was asked, 'What do you think is the most important discovery of your life?' He replied, 'The most important discovery I ever made was when I discovered Jesus Christ.'

In our own day there are a large number of scientists who are professing Christians. The Research Scientist Christian Fellowship has over 200 members and its US counterpart has over 2,000 members. One of the leading scientists of our generation is Revd Dr John Polkinghorne, president of Queens' College, Cambridge, Fellow of the Royal Society, who was professor of mathematical physics before his ordination in 1983. He wrote:

> Men of religion can learn from science what the physical world is really like in its structure and long-evolving history. This constrains what religion can say where it speaks of that world as God's creation. He is clearly a patient God who works through process and not by magic. Men of science can receive from religion a deeper understanding than could be obtained from science alone. The physical world's deep mathematical intelligibility (signs of the Mind behind it) and finely tuned fruitfulness (expressive of divine purpose) are reflections of the fact that it is a creation.[5]

Science and Scripture do not contradict each other

It is probably true that there are more disagreements and apparent contradictions within science itself than between science and the Christian faith. Nevertheless, it is commonly thought that there are conflicts between science and theology.

One of the alleged conflicts is in the area of miracles.[6] Spinoza (1632-1677), the Dutch-Jewish philosopher and the foremost exponent of seventeenth-century rationalism, declared that nothing can 'contravene nature's universal laws'. He believed in a mechanistic uniformity of nature. The philosopher, Hume, regarded a miracle as 'a violation of the laws of nature'[7] and consequently he rejected miracles as being impossible. However, this is a circular argument. If the laws of nature are defined as completely uniform, then the supernatural is ruled out from the start, and it is therefore impossible to believe in miracles, however strong the evidence.

In 1937, the distinguished German physicist, Max Planck, said, 'Faith in miracles must yield ground, step by step, before the steady and firm advance of the forces of science, and its total defeat is indubitably a mere matter of time.'[8] Planck implied that science now explains what was once thought to be miraculous, which suggests that those who believed in miracles in the past, did so because they didn't sufficiently understand the laws of nature. This is not the case. In Jesus' day everyone knew, just as well as we do, that, for example, it is not 'natural' for a virgin to have a baby or for someone to rise from the dead. If they had had no knowledge of the laws of nature, then they would not have recognised a miracle in any shape or form. As C. S. Lewis said, 'Belief in miracles, far from depending on an ignorance of the laws of nature, is only possible insofar as those laws are known.'[9]

The real issue is, 'Is there a God?' If there is, then miracles become a real possibility. If God is God, then he created matter, reason, time, space and all scientific laws, and therefore is at liberty to interfere. If there is no God, then miracles are a problem. But philosophy and science alone will not answer the crucial question. Scientific laws are not laws like the laws of pure mathematics, that cannot be broken. Rather, they are descriptive. As John Stott put it, 'I am not suggesting that miracles are an adequate basis for theism. But, once we have come on other grounds to believe in God . . . it becomes logical to affirm, and illogical to deny, the possibility of the miraculous. For "natural laws" describe God's activity; they do not control it.'[10]

The second area of alleged conflict is the theory of evolution and the biblical account of creation. Is there an irreconcilable conflict?

The first point to note is that much of the theory of evolution is still only theory. It is necessary to distinguish between micro- and macro-evolution. Micro-evolution (which could not conceivably be said to conflict with the Bible) means the variation and development within a species. The horse, for example, has increased greatly in size and developed in other ways over time. This kind of evolution has been observed and there is overwhelming evidence for it.

Macro-evolution, on the other hand, means evolution from one species to another – the most famous example being from apes to humans. It is often thought of as fact, but is still unproved and remains a theory, which is not accepted by all scientists.[11] It is important to stress the provisionality of all scientific theories. The most striking example in modern times is Newtonian physics, which was treated with the utmost respect and regarded as virtually incontestable, until Einstein and others showed that its laws broke down for the very, very small (where Quantum Mechanics becomes relevant) and the very, very fast (where Relativity becomes relevant). Particular versions of theories of evolution are still taught in schools as if they are 'the assured results of modern science'. To regard a scientific theory as more than provisional is bad science.

The second important point is that there are many different interpretations of Genesis held by sincere Christians. Some believe in a literal six-day creation. The Creation Research Society, formed in 1963 as a committee of ten scientists in Michigan, USA, whose membership is limited to scientists having at least a graduate degree in a natural or applied science, now has hundreds of members. They believe that all types of living things were made by direct acts of God during the creation week. Whatever biological changes have occurred since then have been only within the original created kinds.

Other Christians interpret Genesis 1 differently. They point out that the Hebrew word for 'day' has many different meanings, even within Scripture. Since the sun did not appear until day four, the writer probably did not mean twenty-four-hour days. The word can mean a long period of time. Therefore, it is not in conflict with the prevailing scientific view of the vast age of the universe, nor is it in conflict with a gradual evolution in which God not only started the process, but worked within it to produce a system which culminated in human life. They point out that the order of Genesis 1, written by people with no scientific knowledge, is in some ways similar to that accepted by evolutionary theorists, ie, plants, then animals, then man as the climax.

Some add the suggestion that Genesis is about information fed in at intervals ('And God said . . .'). The feeding in of information takes place in a short period of time. The working out of that information takes much longer. They point out that this corresponds remarkably with the theory of the Big Bang, where the essential things happened within the first few minutes.

Many Christians prefer to view Genesis 1 as a literary device, a poetic form, which is not necessarily connected with chronological events in history. It is a pre-scientific and non-scientific account of creation, dealing with matters outside the scope of science. Poetic language can be true without being literally true. When the psalmist wrote, 'The world is firmly established; it cannot be moved' (Psalm 93: 1), he was using a poetic image. But Galileo's opponents took it literally and argued that the earth was stationary and that theories of the earth orbiting the sun were wrong. These Christians feel that in the same way, the early chapters of Genesis should not be taken literally. They say that there is strong evidence for macro-evolutionary theory and that it is now accepted by the vast majority of scientists who argue that the fossil evidence is inconsistent with a literal interpretation of the Genesis account. Those who take this view argue that what matters is that it is God who created and sustains the laws of physics and nature which evolved over time, culminating in human life.

Whichever view one takes, it is clear that there is not necessarily a conflict between science and Scripture. In the light of the uncertainty and the difference of opinions among genuine Christians, I think it is unwise to be too dogmatic about the issue (certainly if, like me, you are neither a scientist nor a theologian).

The main point of Genesis 1 is not to answer the questions 'How?' and 'When?' (the scientific questions), but the questions 'Why?' and 'Who?' (the theological questions). The Bible is not primarily a scientific book, but a theological one. It offers a personal explanation more than a scientific one. The scientific explanation does not prove or disprove the personal one. Rather it is complementary. Even Stephen Hawking, arguably the most brilliant scientist of his generation, has admitted that 'science may solve the problem of how the universe began, but it cannot answer the question: why does the universe bother to exist?'[12]

Dr John Lennox uses the following illustration: 'Suppose I wheel in the most magnificent cake ever seen and I had in front of me various fellows of every academic and learned society in the world and I picked the top men and I tell them to analyse the cake for me. So out steps the world famous nutritionist and he talks about the balance of the various foods that form this cake. Then a leading bio-chemist analyses the cake at the bio-chemical level. Then a chemist says, 'Well, yes, of course, but now we must get down to the very basic chemicals that form this.' Then the physicist comes on and says, 'Well, yes, these people have told you something, but you really need to get down to the electrons and the protons and the quarks.' And last of all the stage is occupied by the mathematician. And he says, 'Ultimately you need to understand the fundamental equations governing the motion of all the electrons and protons in this cake.' And they finish and it is a magnificent analysis of the cake. And then I turn round to them and I say, 'Ladies and Gentlemen, I've just got one more question for you. Tell me *why* the cake was made. And there in front of them stands Aunt Mathilda who made the cake.

It's only when the person who made the cake is prepared to disclose why she's made it that they'll ever understand *why*. No amount of scientific analysis, however exhaustive and detailed, can answer that question.

And then Aunt Mathilda in the end says, 'I'll let you out of your misery. I've made the cake for my nephew Johnny – it's his birthday next week.' And there's the answer, isn't it? No amount of scientific analysis of this planet on which we stand will tell you why it was made unless the Creator chooses himself to speak. The fantastic thing is that he has spoken and what he has spoken is called Genesis.'

Science and Scripture complement each other

God has revealed himself both in creation and supremely in Jesus Christ, as witnessed to in the

Scriptures. Science is the study of God's general revelation in creation. Biblical theology is the study of
God's 'special' revelation in Jesus and the Scriptures.

The psalmist speaks of this general revelation in the
natural world:

> The heavens declare the glory of God;
> the skies proclaim the work of his hands.
> Day after day they pour forth speech;
> night after night they display knowledge.
> There is no speech or language
> where their voice is not heard.
> Their voice goes out into all the earth,
> their words to the ends of the world.
>
> (Psalm 19: 1-4a)

The apostle Paul makes a similar claim: 'For since
the creation of the world God's invisible qualities –
his eternal power and divine nature – have been clearly seen, being understood from what has been made,
so that men are without excuse' (Romans 1: 20; see
also Acts 14: 17; 17: 22-28).

Some have argued, as William Paley did in the
eighteenth century, that the existence of God could be
proved from 'natural theology', ie, God's general revelation in creation. Perhaps that is going too far.
What can be said is that God the Creator has made a
world in which there is much to suggest the presence
of 'more than meets the eye', and he has not left it
wholly without marks of his character.

There are two main arguments for this. First, there
is the argument that since everything has a cause
there must be a first cause. The popular version of
this is in the story of the Hyde Park orator who was
attacking belief in God. He argued that the world just

happened. As he spoke, a soft tomato was thrown at him. 'Who threw that?' he demanded angrily. A Cockney from the back of the crowd replied, 'No one threw it – it threw itself.'

This argument is not a proof, but it is a pointer. It is easier to believe that God created something out of nothing than to believe that nothing created something out of nothing. Towards the end of his life, Charles Darwin wrote of 'the impossibility of conceiving this immense and wonderful universe including man as a result of blind chance or necessity. When thus reflecting, I feel compelled to look to a first cause having an intelligent mind in some degree analogous to that of man and I deserve to be called a theist.'

The second argument is based on the evidence of design. Again, this does not amount to a 'proof', but is a powerful indicator. Professor Chandra Wickramasinghe, who comes from an agnostic Hindu background, has said, 'The chances that life just occurred on earth are about as unlikely as a typhoon blowing through a junkyard and constructing a Boeing 747.'

The matter of design has recently come to the fore with the 'anthropic principle'. The physical constraints of nature are so finely tuned that if they were slightly different, we would not exist.

In the early expansion of the universe there has to be a close balance between the expansive energy (driving things apart) and the force of gravity (pulling things together). If expansion dominated then matter would fly apart too rapidly for condensation into galaxies and stars to take place. Nothing interesting could happen in so thinly spread a world. On the other hand, if gravity dominated the world would collapse in on itself again before there was time for the processes of life to get going. For us to be possible requires a balance between the effects of expansion and contraction which at a very early epoch in the universe's history (the Planck time) has to differ from equality by not more than 1 in 10^{60}. The numerate will marvel at such a degree of accuracy. For the non-numerate I will borrow an illustration from Paul Davies[13] of what that accuracy means. He points out that it is the same as aiming at a target an inch wide on the other side of the observable universe, twenty thousand million light years away, and hitting the mark![14]

Stephen Hawking makes the point that

If the density of the universe one second after the Big Bang had been greater by one part in a thousand billion, the universe would have recollapsed after ten years. On the other hand, if the density of the universe at that time had been less by the same amount, the universe would have been essentially empty since it was about ten years old. How was it that the initial density of the universe was chosen so carefully? Maybe there is some reason why the universe should have precisely the critical density?[15]

Although he does not believe in a creator God, his own theory would seem to point in that direction.

Nor is it just life that has to be explained. It is intelligent life, the human mind, the rational structure of the world, beauty, human love, friendship and justice. These are all dimensions of reality which point beyond chemical and biological laws. Could all this simply be the result of blind chance and natural selection, with no intelligent mind behind the process?

The evidence of science may point to the existence of God. General revelation suggests the tremendous power, intelligence and imagination of a personal creator. But without the special revelation of Jesus Christ as witnessed to in the Scriptures, we would have known little about him.

Albert Einstein, writing from a Jewish perspective, said, 'A legitimate conflict between science and religion cannot exist. Science without religion is lame; religion without science is blind.' Science without religion is lame for a number of reasons. First, we cannot find the God of the Bible through science alone. 'Unfortunately for the scientifically minded, God is not discoverable or demonstrable by purely scientific means. But that really proves nothing; it simply means that the wrong instruments are being used for the job.'[16] We need God's special revelation as well as his general revelation. The first six verses of Psalm 19 speak of God's general revelation. The next verses speak of God's special revelation through his law. It is only through his special revelation that we can find 'the God and Father of our Lord Jesus Christ'.

Secondly, science cannot speak to the deepest needs of men and women. Lewis Wolpert writing in *The Times* said, 'Scientists, or anyone else, without religion, have to face a world in which there is no real purpose, no meaning to torment and joy, and accept that when we are dead we vanish, that there is no after-life.'[17] Science has nothing to say to these deep levels of human experience. It cannot deal with the problem of loneliness or hearts broken by grief. Science is unable to solve the moral dilemmas of humankind. It has no remedy for the problem of unforgiven sin and guilt. Only in the cross of Christ do we find the answer to these problems.

Bestselling novelist, Susan Howatch, had houses in several countries and drove a Porsche and a Mercedes. She said that after the break-up of her marriage, 'God seized me by the scruff of the neck' and she became a Christian. Recently, she gave £1 million to Cambridge University to finance a lectureship in theology and natural science, having come to the conclusion that science and theology were 'two aspects of the truth'. We need science and scientists. Our civilisation owes a great deal to their work. But more than that we need Christianity and we need Jesus Christ.

FOR FURTHER READING

Roger Forster and Paul Marston, *Reason and Faith* (Monarch, 1989).
John Polkinghorne, *One World* (SPCK, 1986).

NOTES

1. C. S. Lewis, *Miracles* (Fontana, 1947) p110.
2. John Polkinghorne, *One World* (SPCK, 1986), p1.
3. John Young, *The Case Against Christ* (Hodder & Stoughton, 1986).
4. John MacMurray, *Reason and Emotion* (Faber), p172.
5. John Polkinghorne, *The Daily Telegraph* (24th August 1992).
6. The term 'miracle' is sometimes used very loosely to describe, for example, remarkable answers to prayer. It is helpful to distinguish 'providence', ie, the guiding or steering by God of nature, humankind and history, from a 'miracle', which has been well-defined by David Atkinson (*The Wings of Refuge* [IVP, 1983], p13) as a 'non-repeatable, counter-instance of an otherwise demonstrable law of nature', eg, walking on water, raising the dead or multiplying food.

7. David Hume, *On Miracles* (1748), p114.

8. Max Planck, *A Scientific Autobiography* (Williams and Norgate, 1950), p155.

9. C. S. Lewis, *Miracles* (Fontana, 1947), p51.

10. John Stott, *Essentials* (Hodder & Stoughton, 1988), p221.

11. Dr James Moore has pointed out that contrary to popular belief it was not the theologians who opposed Darwin as much as the scientists. 'It was few theologians and many scientists who dismissed Darwinism and evolution' (Michael Poole, *Science and Belief* [Lion], p102).

12. Stephen Hawking, *Black Holes and Baby Universes and Other Essays* (Bantam Press, 1993).

13. British physicist Paul Davies, author of *God and the New Physics* and other works, is one of the most popular science writers today. He is notably unsympathetic to conventional Christianity.

14. John Polkinghorne, *One World* (SPCK, 1986), p57.

15. Stephen Hawking, *op cit*.

16. J. B. Phillips, *Gathered Gold* (Evangelical Press, 1984).

17. *The Times* (10th April 1993).

7

Is the Trinity Unbiblical, Unbelievable and Irrelevant?

The word 'Trinity' is derived from the Latin word *trinitas*, which means 'threeness'. Christianity rests on the doctrine of the threeness, the tri-personality, of God. The word 'Trinity' does not appear in the Bible and therefore it is sometimes suggested, particularly by members of cults, that the idea of the Trinity is unbiblical.

Others suggest it is unbelievable because it is incomprehensible. The Athanasian Creed (c. AD 500) sums up the doctrine of the Trinity like this: '. . . that the Father is God, the Son is God and the Holy Ghost is God, and yet there are not three gods, but one God.'

The white queen in Lewis Carroll's *Alice through the Looking Glass* made a habit of believing six impossible things before breakfast. Many wonder whether as Christians we are required to do something similar with the doctrine of the Trinity.

Still others regard the doctrine as an irrelevance. They may believe it is true, but they do not think it is of great importance to their daily lives. Sermons on the Trinity are not exactly crowd-pullers.

Why should we believe in the Trinity? Is it biblical? Is it believable? Is it comprehensible? Is it relevant to our lives today?

Is it biblical?

It is true that the word 'Trinity' does not appear in the Bible. It was first used in its Greek form by an early Christian writer called Theophilus, Bishop of Antioch in c. AD 180. But as Professor F. F. Bruce has remarked, 'Let us not be misled by the foolish argument that because the term "Trinity" does not occur in the scriptures, the doctrine of the Trinity is therefore unscriptural.'

Christianity arose out of Judaism which was a monotheistic faith (Deuteronomy 6: 4) in contrast to the polytheism of the nations which surrounded it. The New Testament itself affirms that there is only one God (John 5: 44; Romans 3: 30; 1 Timothy 1: 17; James 2: 19).

The early Christians were faced with two historical events which revolutionised their understanding of God. First, they were faced with the revelatory events of the life, death and, supremely, the resurrection of Jesus. They came to see that there was something special about Jesus which could only be expressed as

God. They soon found themselves worshipping Jesus as God (eg, John 20: 28) and yet they totally rejected the polytheistic pattern of the Roman world. They came to see him as a man whose identity was God and yet who was not identical to God.

Next, they had an experience of the Holy Spirit which lifted them out of the realms of human experience – one of being caught up in a relationship within the Godhead. They realised that the Holy Spirit was identified with God and Jesus and yet was not identical to either. He was not the Father, nor the Son, but he was one of them. They came to believe in the deity of the Father, the deity of the Son and the deity of the Holy Spirit. Yet they still believed there was only one God.

We can see how John, for example, sets this out in his gospel. He asserts, with the other New Testament writers, that there is only one God (John 5: 44; 17: 3). Yet, in the opening sentences of his gospel he introduces us to two distinct persons within the unity of the Godhead: 'In the beginning was the Word, and the Word was with God, and the Word was God.' As J. I. Packer puts it:

> The Word was a person in fellowship with God, and the Word was himself Personally and eternally divine . . . but this is not all that John means us to learn about the plurality of persons in the Godhead . . . Our Lord (in John's gospel) now gives parallel teaching, to the effect that the divine Spirit is also a person . . . Thus John records our Lord's disclosure of the mystery of the Trinity: three persons, and one God . . . [1]

The concept of the Trinity permeates the pages of the New Testament. Some would say that there are hints of this doctrine, even in the Old Testament, as far back as Genesis 1: 1-3a. In verse 1 we read of God the Creator. In verse 2, 'The Spirit of God was hovering over the waters.' Verse 3 begins, 'And God said . . . .' God created through his Word. John, in his gospel, tells us that the Word is none other than Jesus himself (John 1:14). Thus, God the Father, God the Son and God the Holy Spirit were there at the very beginning.

In the New Testament we find several trinitarian formulae. Baptism is in the name (singular) of the Father and the Son and the Holy Spirit (Matthew 28: 19). Paul ends his second letter to the Corinthians with what we now call 'The Grace': 'May the grace of the Lord Jesus Christ, and the love of God, and the fellowship of the Holy Spirit be with you all' (2 Corinthians 13: 14). While these two texts do not expressly state the doctrine of the Trinity, they point strongly towards it.

Paul sees virtually every aspect of the Christian faith and life in trinitarian terms. As John Stott argues in commenting on Ephesians 1, both halves of the chapter are 'essentially trinitarian . . . both are addressed to God the Father . . . both refer specifically to God's work in and through Christ . . . both sections of the chapter allude – even if obliquely – to the work of the Holy Spirit . . . Christian faith and Christian life are both fundamentally trinitarian'.[2]

In chapter 2 of the same letter, our relationship with God and prayer is seen in trinitarian terms. We pray 'to the Father', through Jesus, 'by one spirit' (Ephesians 2: 18 – for more detailed exposition see *Questions of Life*, Chapter 6). In chapter 3, the filling of the Spirit is described in trinitarian terms, as we shall see later in this chapter. In chapter 4 Christian unity is urged for trinitarian reasons: 'There is . . . one Spirit

. . . one Lord . . . one God and Father of all' (Ephesians 4: 4-6). In his ethical instruction in the second half of Ephesians 4, as John Stott points out, 'It is natural for him, in issuing his moral instructions, to mention the three Persons of the Trinity. He tells us to "copy God", to "learn Christ" and not to "grieve the Holy Spirit".'[3]

Finally, when he refers to our worship, Paul again speaks in trinitarian terms (Ephesians 5: 18-20). 'Once again the doctrine of the Trinity informs and directs our devotion. When we are filled with the Holy Spirit we give thanks to God our Father in the name of the Lord Jesus Christ.'[4]

Nor is Ephesians the only place where Paul's trinitarian thinking emerges. In 1 Corinthians he describes the gifts of the Spirit in this way: 'There are different kinds of gifts, but the same *Spirit*. There are different kinds of service, but the same *Lord*. There are different kinds of working, but the same *God* works all of them in all men' (1 Corinthians 12: 4-6, italics mine).

In 2 Thessalonians Paul sees the Trinity as taking the initiative and providing both the means and goal of salvation: '*God* chose you to be saved through the sanctifying work of *the Spirit* . . . that you might share in the glory of our *Lord Jesus Christ*' (2 Thessalonians 2: 13-14, italics mine).

Paul is not the only trinitarian writer in the New Testament. For example, at the beginning of his first epistle, Peter describes the way we are chosen by God in trinitarian terms: 'To God's elect . . . who have been chosen according to the foreknowledge of *God the Father*, through the sanctifying work of *the Spirit*, for obedience to *Jesus Christ* and sprinkling by his blood' (1 Peter 1: 1-2, italics mine).

In spite of these and many other similar passages in the New Testament, there is no formal credal statement about the Trinity. The early church originally simply experienced the reality of God as Father, Son and Holy Spirit. Only later did she define a coherent and systematic doctrine in response to the heretical views which were being expounded.

On the one hand, for example, Arius (c. 250-336), who was excommunicated from the church for heresy, argued that Jesus was divine but that his divinity was only partial and derivative. The Father, Son and Holy Spirit were three distinct beings. 'The Three he envisages are entirely different beings, not sharing in any way the same nature or essence.'[5] In the sixth century, Philoponus of Alexandria held that there are three gods, who are all of the same sort, and yet distinct and separate from each other. This theology amounts to polytheism.

At the other extreme, Sabellius reduced the Trinity to a unity with three modes of expression. Father, Son and Holy Spirit were no more than symbolic names for one God in his different activities. Instead of three persons, there was one being who changed mask according to whether he was acting as Creator, Redeemer or Sanctifier. There was one person with three names.

Against such heretical views, the council of Constantinople in 381, building on the council of Nicaea in AD 325, spoke of one God (one substance) and three persons. This view of the Trinity has been held by every orthodox church since that time. The traditional doctrine is summed up in the Athanasian Creed:

We worship one God in Trinity, and Trinity in Unity,

neither confounding the Persons nor dividing the Divine Being. For there is one Person of the Father, another of the Son, and another of the Holy Spirit: but the Godhead of the Father, the Son and the Holy Ghost is all one.

Is it believable?

Those who find the doctrine unbelievable because they think it is incomprehensible might point to some other words in the Athanasian Creed: 'The Father incomprehensible, The Son incomprehensible and The Holy Ghost incomprehensible . . . Not three incomprehensibles . . . but . . . one incomprehensible.' As the theologian Alister McGrath points out, many are sorely tempted to add, 'The whole thing incomprehensible!' In fact 'incomprehensible' does not mean 'beyond our understanding'; rather it 'means that the Persons cannot be grasped or pinned down. They cannot be contained or limited by human beings.'[6] Certainly we have to concede that it is not an easy doctrine to understand. We are dealing here with the nature of God himself, so it is not surprising that he stretches the limits of our understanding. One of the greatest theologians of the church, Augustine of Hippo (354-430), wrote fifteen volumes on the Trinity, synthesising and adding the finishing touches to the most profound and exact statements which have ever been made on the subject. Yet even he never delved the full depth of this doctrine. God cannot be put in a neat box and easily understood.

A preacher, speaking on the Trinity, asked the congregation at the end of his sermon, 'Have I made it clear?' One man in the congregation said, 'Yes,' to which the preacher replied, 'In that case you have got it wrong!' St Augustine himself said, 'If you can understand it, it's not God!' He did not mean that we could not or should not seek to understand it, otherwise he would not have written fifteen volumes on the subject. What he meant was that there will always be an element of mystery about God.

In that case one might ask, 'Why bother to try and understand?' and, 'Does it really matter?' The answer is that it does matter and we need to try and understand it as far as we can, because it is fundamental to the Christian faith. Our God is Trinity.

Many have sought human analogies to help us to understand the doctrine. David Prior, the vicar of St Michael's, Chester Square, wrote to *The Times* in June 1992 suggesting a novel analogy:

Last Sunday I dragged myself away from watching the end of the Test match at Lord's in order to preach at our evening service on the theme of 'What Christians believe about the Trinity'. The last three balls I watched being bowled were by Ian Salisbury, England's exciting new spin bowler. The first was a leg-spinner, the second a top-spinner, the third a googly.

I had been ferreting around for a helpful illustration of the Trinity – and there it was: one person expressing himself in three different, but very similar ways. The leg-spinner's stock ball represents God the Father, who created us to 'feel after him'; the top-spinner, which goes straight through, represents the direct activity of God the Son; the googly represents the surprising activity of God the Holy Spirit.[7]

His letter elicited two interesting replies. The first from R. A. Morris who wrote, 'David Prior's trinitarian illustration will have to be called wide. It reflects a serious theological error, identified in the early church as the idea that one God merely *acts* in different ways at different times. Better stick to three stumps in one wicket.'[8] The second from Timothy Russ:

> Perhaps David Prior should have been studying the fathers of the church rather than watching the cricket on Trinity Sunday, for he seems to have expressed very concisely the Sabellian heresy 'one person expressing himself in three different ways', instead of three persons in one substance.   My own anxiety as I dragged myself away from the screen was: 'Will there be anyone at all in church?'[9]

This correspondence illustrates the difficulty in seeking to find an appropriate human analogy.

The most basic analogy is a triangle: three sides but one triangle. Slightly less crude is the shamrock leaf as suggested by St Patrick. Each of the three portions of the leaf is an essential part of that leaf, but the leaf itself is greater than all its parts. In a similar way, the Union Jack is made up of the combination of the flags of St George, St Andrew and St Patrick. Others point to H_2O – which manifests itself as water, ice and steam. The difficulty with all these analogies is that they are impersonal. However, they are illustrative of God's threefold nature. John Eddison, in *Talking to Children*, uses the analogy of a book. A book exists in three different and distinct ways at once – in the mind of the author, on the shelf in the library and in the imagination of the reader. Others use the analogy of a house. The architect (God the Father) can say, 'It's my house.' The purchaser (God the Son) can say, 'It's my house.' And the tenant (God the Spirit) can say, 'It's my house.'[10]

Of course, ideally, an analogy of the Trinity should

be personal. However, there are difficulties with such
analogies. Some have used the parallel of a family
with a father, mother and child. This tends towards
the heresy of Philoponus as it suggests three Gods
and not one. On the other hand, the idea sometimes
used of a father, who is a fireman most of the time, a
footballer on Saturday and a fisherman on Sunday
evening, is Sabellian as it suggests one God with three
modes of expression.

In seeking to understand the Trinity we need to
recognise three limiting factors. First, human language is limited. The Austrian philosopher Ludwig
Wittgenstein pointed out that human words are completely incapable of describing something as mundane as the aroma of coffee. How much more difficult it must be to describe God in human language.

Secondly, we need to recognise the limits of our
own understanding and intellects. 'Our little intellectual systems find themselves groaning under the
strain of trying to accommodate God.'[11] In describing
the Trinity we have to resort to the language of paradox. As defined by the *Concise Oxford Dictionary*, a
paradox is a 'seemingly absurd though perhaps actually well-founded statement'. Scientist and theolo-

gian Alister McGrath gives an example of the paradox from the world of science:

> An example of this from the world of science concerns the nature of light. By the first decade of the twentieth century, it was clear that light behaved in a very strange way – sometimes it seemed to behave as if it was a wave, and sometimes as if it was a particle. It couldn't be both at once, and so the cry 'contradiction!' was raised. How could it be two totally different things? But eventually, through the development of the Quantum Theory, it was found that this contradiction expressed a fundamental difficulty in grasping what the nature of light really was. In other words, the contradiction did not arise on account of light, but on account of our difficulties in conceiving it.[12]

He goes on to show that the nature of light was such that two contradictory models had to be used to account for its behaviour (with God we require three contradictory models).

> Most of us know what light is without needing to think about waves, particles or Quantum Theory. Light is what we need in order to see, to do our everyday business, to read and write. It is what comes out of the sun, and to a lesser extent from the moon. It is what we get when we switch on electric light bulbs or strip lighting. If we were physicists, we might want to think about light in much more detail and go into the full complexities of it – and so we might start talking about waves, particles and Quantum Theory. But we don't need to do this in order to make use of light or to recognize it when we see it.[13]

The fact that we cannot fully comprehend the Trinity does not mean that it does not make sense. When I switch on the television I do not understand how it works, but there is an explanation beyond the limits of my understanding and which does make sense.

Thirdly, we need to recognise the limits of our finite world and our finite minds. C. S. Lewis uses the most helpful analogy I have come across. He writes:

And now, for a few minutes, I must ask you to follow rather carefully.

You know that in space you can move in three ways – to left or right, backwards or forwards, up or down. Every direction is either one of these three or a compromise between them. They are called the three Dimensions. Now notice this. If you are using only one dimension, you could draw only a straight line. If you are using two, you could draw a figure: say, a square. And a square is made up of four straight lines. Now a step further. If you have three dimensions, you can then build what we call a solid body: say, a cube – a thing like a dice or a lump of sugar. And a cube is made up of six squares.

Do you see the point? A world of one dimension would be a straight line. In a two-dimensional world, you still get straight lines, but many lines make one figure. In a three-dimensional world, you still get figures but many figures make one solid body. In other words, as you advance to more real and more complicated levels, you do not leave behind you the things you found on the simpler levels: you still have them, but combined in new ways – in ways you could not imagine if you knew only the simpler levels.

Now the Christian account of God involves just the same principle. The human level is a simple and rather empty level. On the human level one person is one being, and any two persons are two separate beings – just as, in two dimensions (say on a flat sheet of paper) one square is one figure, and any two squares are two separate figures. On the Divine level you still find personalities; but up there you find them combined in new ways which we, who do not live on that level, cannot imagine. In God's dimension, so to speak, you find a being who is three Persons while remaining one Being, just as a cube is six squares while remaining one cube. Of course we cannot fully conceive a Being like that: just as, if we were so made that we perceived only two dimensions in space we could never properly imagine a cube. But we can get a sort of faint notion of it. And when we do, we are then, for the first time in our lives, getting some positive idea, however faint, of something super-personal – something more than a person. It is something we could never have guessed, and yet, once we have been told, one almost feels one ought to have been able to guess it because it fits in so well with all the things we know already.

You may ask, 'If we cannot imagine a three-personal Being, what is the good of talking about Him?' Well, there isn't any good talking about Him. The thing that matters is being actually drawn into that three-personal life, and that may begin any time – to-night, if you like.[14]

Is it relevant?

The doctrine of the Trinity is highly relevant because it sheds light on the nature of God and his interaction with his creation.

First, the Trinity shows that God is self-sufficient. He had no need to create. The three persons of the

Trinity existed before the creation of the universe. God did not need to create in order to love and communicate. The three persons of the Trinity loved each other and communicated with each other before the universe was made.

Secondly, it tells us that

> three essential models must be used if the full depth of the Christian experience and understanding of God is to be expressed adequately. No one picture, image or model of God is good enough – and these three models are essential if the basic outline of our Christian understanding of God is to be preserved. The first model is that of a transcendent God who lies beyond the world as its source and creator; the second is the human face of God, revealed in the person of Jesus Christ; the third is that of the immanent God who is present and active throughout his creation. The doctrine of the Trinity affirms that these three models combine to define the essential Christian insights into the God who raised Jesus Christ from the dead. None of them, taken on its own, is adequate to capture the richness of the Christian experience of God.[15]

Thirdly, it is the triune God who meets our most fundamental psychological needs as human beings. An occupational therapist, trained in psychology in a humanist secular framework, told me that she had been taught that we all need three things. First, we need a point of reference. We need to know who we are, where we have come from and where we are going. Secondly, we need a role model (who might be, for example, a therapist) and thirdly we need a facilitator to help us to get there (this might come from a counsellor or from some group help). When this woman became a Christian she said she realised that God is our point of reference, Jesus is our role model and the Holy Spirit is our facilitator. She saw that the Trinity meets the deepest psychological needs of every human being.

Fourthly, the doctrine of the Trinity is relevant in that it teaches us that there is an inherent threefoldness about every act of God's relevation, which requires us to think in trinitarian terms of the nature of God. In the New Testament virtually every doctrine in experience – baptism, grace, salvation, election, ethics, worship, unity – is described in trinitarian terms. In order to understand God and every doctrine about God we need to think in this way.

I want to end by looking at one example in more detail. In Ephesians 3 Paul describes the fullness of the Spirit in trinitarian terms when he prays that the Ephesian Christians will be filled with the Spirit.

> For this reason I kneel before the Father, from whom his whole family in heaven and on earth derives its name. I pray that out of his glorious riches he may strengthen you with power through his *Spirit* in your inner being, so that *Christ* may dwell in your hearts through faith. And I pray that you, being rooted and established in love, may have power, together with all the saints, to grasp how wide and long and high and deep is the love of Christ, and to know this love that surpasses knowledge – that you may be filled to the measure of all the fulness of *God* (Ephesians 3:14-19, italics mine).

The fullness of the Spirit is an experience of the fatherhood of God. His prayer is to the Father who is the initiator of the process. In Romans 8 Paul speaks more explicitly of the involvement of the Father in the experience of the Spirit, 'because those who are led by the Spirit of God are sons of God. For you did not receive a spirit that makes you a slave again to fear, but you received the Spirit of sonship. And by him we cry, "*Abba*, Father." The Spirit himself testifies with our spirit that we are God's children' (Romans 8:14-16).

It is also an experience of the love of Christ. He prays that 'Christ may dwell in your hearts through faith. And I pray that you, being rooted and established in love, may have power, together with all the saints, to grasp how wide and long and high and deep is the love of Christ, and to know this love that surpasses knowledge – that you may be filled to the measure of all the fulness of God' (Ephesians 3:14-19).

Finally, it is an experience of the power of the Spirit. Paul prays that God would strengthen them 'with power through his Spirit in your inner being' (verse 16). This is the power which Jesus promised to his disciples in his very last words before his ascension (Acts 1: 8).

When the Holy Spirit fills us, we experience the Fatherhood of God, the love of Christ and the power of the Spirit. Yet the three cannot be separated. He prays for 'his Spirit', 'Christ' and 'all the fulness of God' to fill them. The three are in one and one in three. God is not meant only to be understood in our minds but also experienced in our hearts and lives. To be filled with the Spirit is to experience God as Trinity.

FOR FURTHER READING

Alister McGrath, *Understanding the Trinity* (Kingsway Publications, 1987).

NOTES

1. J. I. Packer, *Knowing God* (Hodder & Stoughton, 1973), pp68-70.
2. John Stott, *God's New Society* (IVP, 1979), p52. (Now reissued in the series *The Bible Speaks Today*.)
3. *Ibid*, p191.
4. *Ibid*, p207.
5. J. N. D. Kelly, *Early Christian Doctrines* (Adam and Charles Black, 1960), p229.
6. Gerald Bray, *Creeds, Councils & Christ* (IVP, 1984), p178.
7. *The Times* (25th June 1992).
8. *The Times* (1st July 1992).
9. *Ibid*.
10. John Eddison, *Talking to Children* (H. E. Walter Ltd, 1979), p15.
11. Alister McGrath, *Understanding the Trinity* (Kingsway Publications, 1987).
12. *Ibid*, pp138-139.
13. *Ibid*.
14. C. S. Lewis, *Mere Christianity* (Fount, 1952), pp138-139.
15. Alister McGrath, *op cit*, pp136-137.

Alpha

This book is an Alpha resource. The Alpha course is a practical introduction to the Christian faith initiated by Holy Trinity Brompton in London, and now being run by hundreds of churches throughout the UK as well as overseas. Titles include:

Why Jesus?
A booklet, given to all participants at the start of the Alpha course.
'The clearest, best illustrated and most challenging short presentation of Jesus that I know.' – Michael Green

Questions of Life
The Alpha course in book form. In fifteen compelling chapters Nicky Gumbel points the way to an authentic Christianity which is exciting and relevant to today's world.

Searching Issues
The seven issues most often raised by participants on the Alpha course: suffering, other religions, sex before marriage, the New Age, homosexuality, science and Christianity and the Trinity.

A Life Worth Living
What happens after Alpha? Based on the book of Philippians, this is an invaluable next step for those who have just completed the Alpha course, and for anyone eager to put their faith on a firm biblical footing.

———— ❖ ————

Available from your local Christian bookshop, or through Kingsway Publications, Lottbridge Drove, Eastbourne, E. Sussex BN23 6NT (Freephone 0800 378446). For more information on Alpha, and details of tapes, videos and training manuals, contact the Alpha office, Holy Trinity Brompton on 071-581 8255, or STL, PO Box 300, Kingstown Broadway, Carlisle, Cumbria CA3 0QS.

Alpha Hotline for telephone orders:
0345 581278 (all calls at local rate)

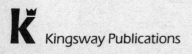

Kingsway Publications

Alpha